Promising Partnerships

Ways to Involve Parents in Their Children's Education

Lisa J. Harpin

ROWMAN & LITTLEFIELD EDUCATION
A division of
ROWMAN & LITTLEFIELD PUBLISHERS, INC.
Lanham • New York • Toronto • Plymouth, UK

Published by Rowman & Littlefield Education
A division of Rowman & Littlefield Publishers, Inc.
A wholly owned subsidiary of The Rowman & Littlefield Publishing Group, Inc.
4501 Forbes Boulevard, Suite 200, Lanham, Maryland 20706
www.lexingtonbooks.com

Estover Road, Plymouth PL6 7PY, United Kingdom

British Library Cataloguing in Publication Information Available

Library of Congress Cataloging-in-Publication Data

Harpin, Lisa J., 1960-
   Promising partnerships : ways to involve parents in their children's education / Lisa J. Harpin.
      p. cm.
   Includes bibliographical references.
   ISBN 978-1-60709-562-0 (cloth : alk. paper) — ISBN 978-1-60709-563-7 (pbk. : alk. paper) — ISBN 978-1-60709-564-4 (electronic)
   1. Education—Parent participation. 2. Parent-teacher relationships. I. Title.
   LB1048.5.H366 2010
   371.19'2—dc22   2010030013

∞™ The paper used in this publication meets the minimum requirements of American National Standard for Information Sciences—Permanence of Paper for Printed Library Materials, ANSI/NISO Z39.48-1992.

Printed in the United States of America

To educators and parents everywhere who join together to form partnerships that inspire children to succeed with promising results.

Table of Contents

Educators, families, community members, and students are partners in education. They share responsibility for children's success in school at all grade levels. As partners, they must work together to create excellent schools and to support student learning.

—Epstein et al., 2009

Introduction

As educators, we recognize the importance and challenge of strengthening parent involvement in education. Study after study reveals that engaging parents in their children's education will ultimately lead to improved student achievement.

Education has grossly changed over the years, and the twenty-first century calls for new paradigms for parent involvement that move away from the century-old model where schools operated like factories and rarely invited parent input or participation.

With the passing of the No Child Left Behind Act of 2001, schools are now required to create and implement ways for parents to be involved in the schools. This law was initially created to close the achievement gap between disadvantaged and minority students and their peers by improving the public schools to increase teaching and learning. It is based upon four basic principles that include stronger accountability for results, increased flexibility and local control, expanded options for parents, and emphasis on proven teaching methods.

This is no easy task for educators or parents. As states, districts, and schools grapple for ways to engage greater numbers of parents in their children's education, many find it difficult to increase the number of parents and types of parental involvement. This seems to be especially difficult among schools serving low-income and limited English proficient populations where a number of reasons may influence the lack of parent involvement.

The families in these schools may be experiencing difficult circumstances, parents' own negative educational experiences as students, language barriers, and immigrant parents who feel insecure about questioning educators because of cultural beliefs. Many parents have little knowledge about how to become involved in their child's education and feel incapable of contributing in meaningful ways. Others simply feel unwelcome to do so.

Parents require encouragement, information, and specific training to become involved, but districts are not always in the position to provide these elements. Parent involvement in education can take many forms. Typically, we expect a child's education to begin in the home with parents providing a caring and healthy environment that is filled with developmentally appropriate learning experiences. When a child enters school, research suggests that the most effective parental involvement seems to occur when it is looked upon as a partnership between parents and educators.

After reviewing much of the literature related to parent involvement in the schools, I discovered a great deal of research that supports parental involvement and its positive correlation with increased student achievement. Further, a host of resources and activities exist that are designed to engage parents in their child's education. I have not, however, come across a publication that unifies the stakeholders involved and ties all of the necessary elements together in a text that can be utilized by parents and school districts.

I have attempted to make this possible by authoring *Promising Partnerships*. Backed by the current research and personal experience, I attempted to address the challenges that the major stakeholders face in forming a promising partnership (the educators, the parents, and the students themselves) and to offer the knowledge, best practices, and solutions to meet them.

This book is organized into thematic chapters. Each chapter is divided into two segments: "Essentials for Educators" and "Practices for Parents."

- "Essentials for Educators" provides school personnel with information regarding theory and practice in the area of parental education. Information is also provided for educators to use to form important connections with families, such as how to implement a family literacy night.
- "Practices for Parents" provides parents with the means to make important connections with their children and their children's school.

When appropriate, supports for students are included in chapters that contain a topic useful to students directly. The intent is to provide schools and parents with a practical and useful tool to address the current need for parental engagement in the education process and to ultimately form promising partnerships among those involved.

Lisa J. Harpin, Ed.D.

Chapter 1

Back to School Success: How to Best Prepare for the Year Ahead

There is no doubt about it; going back to school can be a challenge for children and their parents. Children have to adjust to new teachers, schedules, classrooms, and sometimes even schools. Parents have the responsibility of helping their children with these adjustments, along with establishing a routine that will promote school success.

Family involvement affects student achievement in a number of ways. A strong correlation exists between family involvement and student achievement that suggests the greater the involvement, the higher the student achievement. Students achieve higher grades and test scores, have better attendance records, and complete homework on a more regular basis when parents share an interest in their academics. These students achieve higher graduation rates and are more likely to take part in postsecondary education. Positive attitudes and behavior are more evident, and these students are less likely to engage in drug and alcohol use or violent behaviors when there is evidence of strong family involvement.

Significant benefits for all ages and grade levels result when parents become involved in their children's education, regardless of socioeconomic status, ethnic/racial background, or parents' level of education. More importantly, they result from a home environment that values learning, encourages two-way communication, and participates in educational experiences at home and in the community. Educators respect and have a higher regard for parents and families who are actively involved in the educational process, and they have higher expectations for the children of these families.

Schools desire to form partnerships with parents that foster collaboration among those involved. Many times, the achievement of disadvantaged children and children who are trailing behind improves significantly with

3

programs in place designed to involve parents in full partnerships. This holds
true for children from diverse cultural backgrounds, especially when educators attempt to close the gap between the home culture and the school culture.
In order to have the strongest impact on these children, parental involvement
activities must be planned well, all-encompassing, and designed to reach the
targeted population.

Parental involvement cannot cease after the elementary school years.
Middle and high school students whose parents remain connected transition
better, retain quality work habits, and form goals and plans for the future, and
they are less likely to drop out of school. When schools and families work
together to support learning, the children are apt to succeed not only in school
but also throughout life.

Although parents may want to be involved with their children's education,
they may be unaware or unsure of the ways to do so. Factors such as cultural
barriers, fear of authority-based institutions, parental illiteracy, family problems, and negative educational experiences play a large role in a parent's lack
of involvement. Job-related issues, economic conditions, health, living arrangements, and lack of resources also impact the degree of parent involvement.

Teachers and school administrators can generate a number of opportunities
that improve communication and raise a parent's comfort level and willingness to participate in a child's education at home and at school. This chapter
is designed to provide suggestions that promote parental involvement in the
school. It will also serve to furnish parents with ways they can interact with
each other, their children's teachers, and their own children.

ESSENTIALS FOR EDUCATORS

For starters, districts can initiate parental involvement by developing a
written policy that validates the importance of this relationship. Administrators, teachers, and parents should join forces in developing the policy. Goal
setting, the definition of roles, needs sensing, and the setting of school standards should be developed as partners, along with evaluation criteria for the
successfulness of the policy.

Partnerships tend to weaken when there is an absence of clearly stated
criteria about how those involved will support the shared mission with clearly
defined roles of the partners. Once a partnership has been established, the
members need to commit to collaborating on a regular basis. When information is withheld, the partnership may be negatively affected.

When establishing new partnerships, new educators should be encouraged
to convey their needs. For true collaboration to happen, all parties should

mutually decide on the roles and responsibilities. Periodic meeting times are necessary to evaluate the partnership and review expectations, whether the partnership involves parents or members of the community.

With communication as a key factor in promoting parental involvement, school districts must seek ways to make this happen. Because little to no training is provided to teachers in ways to involve parents in their children's education, it is recommended that districts utilize in-service days or professional development sessions to train teachers in such areas as effective parent-teacher conferences, telephone conversations, e-mail communications, and parent newsletters. These methods will be especially helpful to novice teachers. With constricting school budgets, districts should seek out businesses and community organizations for monetary and service support so that effective partnerships can form and sustain themselves over time.

The Scituate School District, located in Scituate, Rhode Island, has worked hard to create a parental involvement component devoted to utilizing the most meaningful methods to ensure that parents are engaged in their children's education while complying with Title I regulations.

The Scituate School District acknowledges the importance of parental involvement in the education of all children. The district believes that, when parents play an active role in their children's education, everyone reaps the benefits. Most importantly, children receive a strong message that parents believe education has a significant impact on their future.

With this in mind, the district developed its own policy to address parental involvement as a necessary component of each child's education. The district reviewed the research on parental involvement in the schools. After much dialogue with administrators, teachers, parents, and members of the community, the district's Title I Parental Involvement Policy was drafted and accepted.

The concept of parental involvement is also embedded in the district's strategic plan. By doing so, all members in the district take the policy for parental involvement seriously, and more opportunities exist for parents to become engaged in their children's education. Parents and members of the community are viewed as important contributors to the educational process and vital to the success of the district's mission to provide students with the knowledge and skills to become responsible, successful, contributing citizens.

The following components represent the core of the district's Title I Parental Involvement Policy. They encompass the best theory and practice and encourage educational/parental partnerships.

• Shared Responsibilities for High Student Academic Achievement involves a compact developed with parents that outlines how parents, educators, and students share in the responsibility for improved academic achievement.

The vehicles to make this happen include the distribution of the policy to all families, an annual parent conference, frequent progress reports, accessibility to staff, parental opportunities to volunteer, and surveys to gauge the effectiveness of the policy.

- Building Capacity for Involvement supports a partnership between the school community and the parent community to improve academic achievement. This is accomplished by providing assistance for parents to obtain an understanding of topics such as state standards, state assessments, and Title I requirements. Parents are also advised on how to monitor their child's progress and work with educators to improve academic achievement through workshops, conferences, PTA meetings, school improvement team meetings, and parent resource centers. Educators are provided with professional development experiences aimed at valuing the contributions of parents, communicating with parents, coordinating and implementing parent programs, and working with parents as partners.
- Accessibility allows schools to provide opportunities for the parents with limited English proficiency, disabilities, and of migratory children to participate in the educational process. These parents receive school-related information and reports in a format and language that can be understood. Software technology to translate documents is available for families. In addition, every effort is made to accommodate parents by varying times and locations when setting up meetings. The district organizes an annual meeting to explain the Parental Involvement Policy and offers opportunities for involvement. The meeting also serves as a vehicle to receive feedback on the policy's success. Throughout the school year, parents continue to be updated on the policy, curriculum, interventions, and assessments through e-mails, newsletters, parent-teacher conferences, and personal contacts.

It is evident that the Scituate School District believes that education is a shared responsibility of the home, school, and community. They have created and implemented a parental involvement policy that incorporates best practice, is realistic, invites input from stakeholders, and is doable for those involved. These are important elements to keep in mind when districts are crafting parental involvement policies.

Many factors influence both parent and community involvement in the schools. Three related elements are of particular importance: communication, participation, and governance.

Two-way communication that extends to and from parents and the community can be established with newsletters, telephone calls, home visits, parent-teacher conferences, and e-mail.

Participation assesses the extent to which parents and members of the community are involved in the day-to-day operation of the school and suggests the use of parent and community volunteers in a variety of capacities. Such volunteers can assist classroom teachers, help with clerical needs, and act as guest lecturers or presenters in their areas of expertise.

The concept of governance takes into account the established structures within a school that allow parents and members of the community to participate in decision-making practices relative to school policy. One vehicle for promoting governance is the school's school improvement team. Parents should be notified of the school improvement team's purpose, meeting times, and the many valuable contributions that they can lend by becoming an active member.

The concept of parent involvement has long been studied, but few models exist that offer the necessary elements to unify educators and parents. Joyce Epstein at Johns Hopkins University developed a framework that outlines six types of parent and community involvement. Her research-based model includes components that bridge the gap between parents and the school. The components are outlined as follows

Parenting
- Creating home environments that support children as students is essential. It is important for educators to assist families in establishing such an environment through vehicles such as parent education, family support programs, and home visits, if possible, when the child transitions from one educational setting to another.

Communicating
- School-to-home and home-to-school communication is necessary. Communication that effectively conveys children's educational performance through conferencing, useful notes, memos, telephone calls, and newsletters on a regular basis needs to be developed and maintained.

Volunteering
- Parents need to be called upon for help and support through volunteer programs. The creation of parent and family centers is also a good way to promote involvement. Surveys are recommended to assess the talents and interests of parents as well as their availability.

Learning at Home
- The skills and knowledge base that parents need in order to help their children at home need to be identified. Parents should be taught how to become involved in academic activities such as helping with homework and other curriculum-related decisions.

Decision Making
• The forums that are available for parents to become involved in—as well
  as the decisions that would be appropriate for parents to participate in—
  should be assessed. Organizations such as the PTO/PTA, advisory councils,
  school improvement teams, advocacy groups, and parent-family networks
  are possibilities.

Collaborating with Community
• Community services exist that strengthen student learning, school programs, and family practices. Services and programs involving community
  health; cultural, recreational, and social support services; summer programs; and ways that families, students, and schools can give to the community are most beneficial.

Schools need not undertake the task of increasing parent involvement single-
handedly. State and district support are necessary to successfully implement
such an initiative.

In 2002, the National Association of State Boards of Education (NASBE)
produced a document entitled "From Sanctions to Solutions: Meeting the
Needs of Low-Performing Schools." It is a result of the work completed by
a study group that examined the current status of low-performing schools
across the United States and delineated how state policies can identify
financial, human, and programmatic resources to transform low-performing
schools.

One piece that was looked at concerned ways in which state and district
actions could support parent involvement in schools. The efforts of the study
group resulted in the following support system.

District Actions to Support Effective Parent Involvement Programs
1. Ensure that school personnel develop cultural competency to help support
   meaningful parent and community involvement.
2. Arrange for schools that are trying to establish effective parent involvement programs to visit schools that already have them.
3. Make measures of parent involvement a part of the school accountability
   system.
4. Provide technical assistance to school leaders in the area of parent involvement.

State Actions to Support Effective Parent Involvement Programs
1. Include parent involvement strategies and the importance of parent
   involvement in teacher and leadership preparation programs.

2. Forge partnerships with state-level parent organizations.
3. Provide information to schools and districts about promising practices.
4. Ensure that staff members at the state education agency support parent involvement and build the idea of parents as a resource into state mission statements and goals.

The district actions identified can be adapted to meet the needs of a particular school district and integrated. The state actions that seem most beneficial for a school district can be accomplished if educators lobby and communicate with senators and representatives until they recognize the importance of such actions, too.

School districts have the tremendous responsibility of improving low-performing schools and maintaining high-performing schools. Educators should not work alone to accomplish these tasks. Their work can be achieved more effectively by involving families, communities, and other social service agencies.

PRACTICES FOR PARENTS

Children can reach their full academic potential by having parents who are interested and involved in their academic progress. Many parents have different ideas of how they fit into their child's education. These ideas can differ greatly from those of a teacher, school, or district.

The benefits that parents will receive when involved in their child's education are rewarding. These benefits include a greater appreciation for their role as a parent, a greater sense of adequacy and self-worth, stronger social networks, and an interest in possibly continuing their own education.

The following list may serve as a starting point for parents to utilize when beginning their involvement in education. These suggestions are intended to assist parents in strengthening a relationship with their children and their children's teachers.

Encourage Your Child to Read
- Get the whole family involved.
- Act as a reading role model. Let your children see you reading.
- Go to the library and take your children with you. Encourage them to apply for a library card.
- Search for ways to teach your children to love stories and storytelling. Tell them stories about their own family and their culture.

Help Your Children to Become Familiar with Vocabulary That Will Benefit
Them in Life
- Identify important and helpful words at places like the market, pharmacy,
gas station, bank, and so forth.

Improve Your Children's Writing/Communication Skills
- Encourage them to write letters and thank-you notes.
- Encourage e-mails and telephone calls with a specific and meaningful
purpose.

Improve Your Children's Math Skills
- When visiting various stores, have them add up the prices as you shop.
- Teach your children to estimate the cost of the shopping while you are add-
ing items to the shopping cart.

Play Learning Games with Your Children
- Find a word in a thesaurus and see who can list the most synonyms.
- Read newspaper articles together to determine the five Ws (who, what,
when, where, and why).

Use TV Time Wisely
- Remember that children who watch more than ten hours of television per
week or an average of two hours per day decline academically.
- Select educational programs. Watch and discuss television shows together.

Take the Time to Talk with Your Children
- Ask them questions about school and their schoolwork, like, "What was the
most important thing you learned today? What new assignments did you
get? What do you think your teacher will ask you on the test?"

Monitor Your Children's Schoolwork
- Check their assignment pads/student planners each day.
- Establish a scheduled homework time.
- Ask questions about homework.
- Check homework over to be sure it has been completed.
- Review material for upcoming tests with them.

Monitor Activities and After-School Jobs
- Be sure that your children are not spending too many hours with things that
may interfere with schoolwork.
- Limit watching TV, playing computer games, or talking on the telephone.

Attend Parent Conferences and Parents' Nights
- Read school newsletters sent home.
- Familiarize yourself with and use your children's school website.
- Consider joining organizations for parents.

Send a Message to Your Children That School Is Important
- Find ways to show your children you are proud of them when they do the best they can.
- Express high expectations for your children. Encourage them to work to their full potential and meet challenges.
- Encourage regular school attendance. Allow your children to stay home for serious illness or only when necessary.
- Show respect for your children's teachers by not criticizing a teacher in front of them.

Encourage Healthy Habits
- Be sure that your children get enough sleep.
- Be sure that your children eat three square meals each day.
- Provide healthy snacks in between meals.
- Be sure that your children have some exercise time built into their day.

HOMEWORK TIPS

The benefits of homework have long been debated, yet most educators will agree that homework does more good than bad. When homework is meaningful, it can improve students' study skills, create more positive attitudes toward school, and help students to discover that learning can take place outside of the school.

Homework has nonacademic benefits, too. It can foster independence and responsibility. Parents who are involved with their children's homework develop a stronger appreciation of education and communicate positive attitudes toward their children's achievements and accomplishments.

Essentials for Educators

In order for students to experience academic success, they must take personal responsibility for their own learning. Part of that responsibility includes coming to school prepared for work and completing homework assignments on a daily basis. One way for educators to foster these responsibilities is to offer opportunities for students to work on assignments and homework that extend beyond the school day. Four worthwhile after-school services provided by one Ohio middle school are worth sharing.

One service includes after-school academic sessions offered by teachers Tuesday through Friday for one hour, for modified small group instruction. These sessions are scheduled after working closely with teachers and the teachers' union.

The school also houses a homework center that is staffed by two teachers who are compensated for operating the center, which extends beyond the after-school academic sessions.

In addition, a twenty-four-hour homework hotline has been established as a service to students and parents. Teachers can record their assignments on the hotline from school or home. Through a monthly newsletter, parents and students are provided with a list of teachers' access codes.

Lastly, the school has partnered with a local university. Middle school students are partnered with university sophomores and juniors to receive individual tutoring in certain subject areas. Tutoring sessions take place during the after-school academic sessions.

Joyce Epstein created Teachers Involve Parents in Schoolwork (TIPS) to involve parents in the completion of homework assignments. TIPS interactive homework assignments require students to talk to someone at home about something they are learning about in school. TIPS activities should contain meaningful curriculum content, involve realistic student responsibilities, and encourage productive family interactions.

A student's developmental level and the quality of his or her home support should govern the amount and the kind of homework assigned. Many educators refer to the ten-minute rule when determining homework tasks. The ten-minute rule dictates that ten minutes be multiplied by the student's grade level to calculate the amount of time the homework should be designed for. A child in the first grade, for example, should receive ten minutes of homework, while a child in the sixth grade should receive sixty minutes of homework.

Homework has an overall positive effect on student achievement. It should be structured with time limits that relate to a child's grade level. It should have a well-articulated purpose and relate directly to learning goals. Educators are urged to provide guidelines for parents that specify how they can assist their children with homework tasks. The following section offers a set of guidelines for parents to utilize.

Practices for Parents

Homework completion can be a challenge at home. Oftentimes, parents have difficulty knowing just where to begin to help their children with their schoolwork. A busy work schedule for parents, numerous after-school activities for children, and a lack of academic resources in the home are some of the obstacles families face when confronted by homework.

The following simple guidelines may help to make homework completion at home a little easier and more meaningful for parents and children:

- Establish a structured homework routine with a scheduled homework time. Use the idea of same time, same place, each day.
- Establish a homework station free from distractions.
- Create a homework toolbox with supplies such as paper, pens, pencils, rulers, calculators, and so forth.
- Gather resources such as a dictionary, thesaurus, and a computer with Internet access if possible.
- Offer guidance and support without actually completing the homework for your children.
- Check homework assignments over to be sure they have been completed correctly.
- If your children state that they have no homework, have them still use the homework time to read, write in a journal, or study material for upcoming tests.
- Provide your children with notebooks and folders that will help with the transportation and organization of homework assignments.
- Encourage your children to use a special assignment pad or student planner daily to record homework and upcoming tests. Check it daily with your children.
- If your children's teachers post assignments and important information on a website, check the site daily with your children, if you have Internet access.

Helpful Homework Websites

The Internet is a powerful tool for parents, students, and educators. Numerous websites exist and serve as a resource rich with information and suggestions to help with the completion of homework. Many offer actual lessons with multimedia enhancements such as interactive animations, audio and video lessons, quizzes, and exercises. Others provide homework aid for all ages such as interactive tutorials, information sites on numerous topics, and e-mail help sites. Still others offer a study web to search for or browse through topics.

Useful Parent Internet Sites

The Internet, likewise, offers information to address a host of parent-related issues that stem from a parent's desire to understand his or her role in the child's education. Many of these sites teach parents how to become involved in the educational process and stay connected. Others provide parents with resources to help their children academically, such as appropriate age-level books and how to access them. Still other sites extend beyond the realm of academics and show parents what to expect as their child grows developmentally and emotionally. Parents can also access activities to engage in and places to go with their children.

Student achievement increases when collaboration exists among educators, parents, and the community. To address the challenge of making this happen, educators must reach out to parents and the community to form lasting partnerships that have positive effects on students.

Chapter 2

Test-Taking

We live in a world where test-taking has become a way of life for young people. Many things depend upon how well students perform on tests, and the pressure is great to excel on the tests they are required to take. Educational and career opportunities are two of the most important areas influenced by test results. In comparison to other industrialized nations, American students make up the largest population of students tested, and the repertoire of tests is great. Throughout their educational career, students are exposed to teacher-made tests, district tests, state tests, entrance exams, exit exams, specialized subject tests, and national standardized tests.

With the passing of the No Child Left Behind (NCLB) Act of 2001 came the birth of high-stakes tests. The act also produced the mindset that raising standards and high-stakes testing would improve teaching and learning, motivate students to achieve, and decrease the dropout rate. Evidence shows that the opposite is occurring. While students are scoring better on high-stakes tests, they are failing to improve in other areas such as motivation, and the dropout rate is increasing, especially in states where the stakes are highest.

Schools are now required to be accountable according to NCLB. Schools must test students in grades two through twelve in the areas of reading, math, and science. Each state is allowed to choose its own test and standards of proficiency. Schools that do not demonstrate "adequate yearly progress" toward achieving proficiency suffer federal sanctions, such as losing federal funding, providing free tutoring, and allowing students to transfer to another school. If improvement still fails to occur, a complete restructuring of the school will take place.

NCLB has prompted educators to work toward aligning instruction, curriculum, standards, and assessment so teachers and students obtain a clear understanding of what should be taught and learned. States are expected to provide resources and curriculum that match the standards, and the tests measure achievement of the standards. Districts must meet the criteria for having strong content standards, and they must document the tests that students take align with the standards specifically in grades three through twelve in the areas of reading and mathematics.

High-stakes testing, as well as other forms of testing, are here to stay. Along with them comes a great deal of test anxiety for students, educators, and parents to some degree. One of the most effective ways to deal with the subject of testing and the ramifications is to help students understand the relevance of testing and form connections between what they are asked to learn and why they are being tested on it.

This chapter will inform educators of the best practices to use to prepare students for taking tests and inspire them to do well when completing them. This chapter will also help parents to recognize the role that tests play in their children's education. It offers advice to parents for conveying a positive attitude toward testing and encouraging children to attempt their best effort without pressure. Finally, a large portion of this chapter will offer test-taking strategies that students themselves may draw from to lower their test-taking anxiety and perform in the best way they know how.

ESSENTIALS FOR EDUCATORS

Many factors influence a student's ability to become a skillful test-taker. At the start of each school year, teachers should provide students with the methods needed for a successful school year. Helpful methods include strategies for completing homework assignments, reviewing study material, and reading for school or pleasure. It is imperative that test-taking skills be added to the list of strategies.

Students should receive notification and be given sufficient time to prepare for a test. They should have access to study materials related to the topic being assessed, and the material should be reviewed frequently in class. Study guides are useful tools. It is essential that students understand the purpose of the assessment. When students are aware of the reasons for the testing, they are more likely to work to the best of their ability. It provides a connection between content and assessment for students.

Students with special needs should be provided with accommodations during testing situations. These students may require a test setting free of distractions, additional time to complete tests, oral testing, or an individual to scribe answers.

One of the best pieces of advice that educators can relay to students is that tests should not be feared, but should be taken seriously. The purpose of most tests is to determine a student's strengths and weaknesses. Educators should assure students that areas of weakness will be remediated in some way. Test results should always be shared and explained to students.

A large part of what happens in a student's future results from the scores he or she receives on high-stakes standardized tests. The reputations of our nation's schools and their educators are also at the mercy of test scores. Because of this, districts are encouraging their teachers to "teach to the test." A vast difference exists between teaching to the test and instilling test-taking strategies in students. Teaching to the test focuses on the content of the subject to be tested. Teaching test-taking strategies adds to a student's understanding of test format and the conventions of a specific type of test.

A great deal of controversy surrounds the concept of teaching to the test. Many educators see it as a way of narrowing the curriculum to better focus on the subject matter being tested. Changes are made to match the test both in content and method of instruction. Educators concentrate heavily on memorization of isolated facts rather than developing higher-order abilities and design assessments in a multiple-choice fashion. Although increased test scores have been noted as a result of utilizing methods such as teaching to the test, this does not substantiate improvement in real academic performance.

The United States tends to rely heavily on multiple-choice tests while other nations have engaged in more performance-based assessments. Interestingly, these students tend to score better on multiple-choice tests than students in the United States who are trained to take tests in this manner. The United States, however, is making great strides in the area of performance-based assessment where students are evaluated on the basis of real work such as essays, projects, and activities that are authentic in nature.

Years of research demonstrate the positive effects of teaching students to be test-wise. Learning test-taking strategies will make students more confident in testing situations. Test scores will more accurately reflect the degree of knowledge of a particular subject a student knows or does not know, and a lack of knowledge will not be the result of being intimidated by the test. When test scores indicate a student's true knowledge base, it improves the validity of the test because the test measures what it is supposed to measure.

A majority of students have experienced some degree of test anxiety. It is present in all populations and age groups. Nearly 20 percent of teens experience test anxiety, but, with today's high-stakes testing, this kind of anxiety is channeling down to even younger students. It can result from a number of factors. A prior negative experience during a test can impact future test-taking. Lack of preparation, poor study habits, lack of organization, and poor time management can also contribute to test anxiety. Still other factors may include lack of confidence, fear of failure, and fear that the results will negatively influence the future. When test anxiety is high, students may spend greater amounts of time worrying about the negative consequences of a test than on the test preparation itself to succeed.

Test anxiety produces noticeable symptoms that affect an individual's overall health. Physical symptoms include headaches, nausea or diarrhea, extreme body temperature changes, excessive sweating, shortness of breath, lightheadedness or fainting, rapid heartbeat, and dry mouth. Emotionally, students may suffer from excessive feelings of fear, disappointment, anger, depression, uncontrollable crying or laughing, and feelings of helplessness.

In the behavioral realm, fidgeting, pacing, substance abuse, and avoidance can be witnessed. Students' cognitive functioning may also be affected. They may experience racing thoughts, fear of going blank during the test, difficulty concentrating, negative thoughts about themselves, feelings of dread, difficulty organizing thoughts, and the desire to compare themselves to others.

In many cases, students' self-worth and self-esteem suffer enormously from poor test results, and test anxiety escalates. High degrees of test anxiety can interfere with learning and lead to poor performance.

Educators can assist in reducing test anxiety by adequately preparing students for upcoming tests in class and providing them with study guides and materials that can be used at home. They can notify parents of upcoming tests through student planners, school websites, and secure Internet websites that allow educators to publicize information.

If parents are aware of the subjects being tested and are supplied with study materials, they are more likely to assist their children at home. This will reinforce the subject matter, enhance the overall learning experience, and ultimately give students the confidence they need to succeed.

Educators and parents can influence the degree of test anxiety a student experiences. Placing the concept of test-taking into perspective is the first step in reducing test anxiety. Students should be encouraged to do their best. They should be offered support rather than overwhelming expectations or threatening consequences. It is reasonable to be concerned about a test without causing unnecessary test anxiety.

Students who suffer from test anxiety worry about being successful in school. They can be extremely self-critical, lose their self-confidence, and feel incompetent. All of these feelings can extend over many academic areas and disable students from succeeding in many aspects of the educational process.

PRACTICES FOR PARENTS

Parents are their children's first teachers. They are pivotal in the academic success of their children. It is important for parents to be aware of the many factors that influence their children's success in school. One of the most important factors is testing.

Test results can be the deciding factor in many aspects of your child's education. Your child's placement, remediation eligibility, grade promotion and retention, and college acceptance are just a few areas in which test results have a substantial influence. Although testing can be a challenging experience, certain strategies can be utilized to make the situation somewhat less threatening. Parents need to maintain a positive attitude toward testing and recognize that test results are not the only means to gauge a child's achievement in school; they are just one measure of a child's strengths and weaknesses.

Parents are advised to encourage their children to do well on a test without needless pressure. It can be difficult to achieve this balance. It is important for children to feel relaxed before, during, and after a test to create a positive experience that will transcend over future testing situations. Taking the time to practice test-taking strategies at home will help to accomplish this. The following is a list of suggestions that will help children improve their test scores and test-taking ability.

- Before a test, make a plan for academic success. Review your child's current study habits and discuss ways to improve them.
- Frequently review the subject matter for upcoming tests together. To avoid cramming the night before a test, be sure your child spaces out the time spent on completing homework and the time spent studying for tests.
- Take advantage of study guides and materials sent home by teachers, and use them to help your child prepare for tests.
- Have your child take frequent breaks while studying and completing complicated homework assignments.
- Keep track of upcoming tests on a calendar as a reminder for you and your child.
- Provide a well-lit study area that is free of distractions to help your child study effectively.
- If you feel anxious about your child's test, try to keep calm around your child.
- Before every test, recognize it is essential that your child get a good night's sleep. Brains do not function well when they are sleep-deprived.
- Provide your child with a healthy breakfast on the morning of the test. Serve whole-grain cereals along with lean protein, such as eggs, to help your child maintain energy and stay alert during a test.

- Studies have shown that young people experience physical effects from hunger such as headaches, stomach pain, and sleepiness. They can also become restless and inattentive by late morning.
- Allow your child to dress comfortably on the day of the test.
- Be sure your child wakes up early enough on the day of a test to arrive at school on time. Being late on the day of a test will cause unnecessary anxiety.
- Offer words of praise, support, and encouragement as your child heads out the door on the morning of a test. Avoid words that may cause your child to feel pressured.
- Suggest relaxation exercises such as deep breathing before a test begins.
- Instruct your child to read test directions carefully and to ask questions if something is not clear.
- Advise your child to complete the easiest test items first and then tackle the rest.
- Remind your child to carefully check over responses to test items before turning in the test.
- Maintain a positive attitude about tests. Tell your child that it is important to want to do well on a test, but one test will not measure all that an individual can do.
- Praise and reward your child when he or she does well on a test, and encourage him or her to do better when he or she does poorly.
- Although most teachers will review mistakes with students when they return tests, ask your child to bring tests home so you can look over the test and discuss the errors with your child.
- If your child appears to be struggling with tests and receiving poor grades, meet with teachers to discuss ways to help your child at home.

Tests are important, especially for schoolchildren. Tests can also be found in everyday life experiences. Obtaining a driver's license, qualifying for sports, or securing a job are just a few. Schools use tests to assess and improve education. Tests tell educators what to do to improve courses and curriculum so students will be successful and prepared for life's experiences.

All tests reveal how students are performing. Most tests that young people experience are teacher-made and associated with the grades that students receive on a report card. They measure students' strengths and weaknesses and alert educators of the areas students excel in and the areas students need help in.

Standardized tests also assess students' strengths and weaknesses. These tests, however, measure student performance across the country. They compare each student's test results with that of others in the same grade and age group who took the same test.

Regardless of the type of test, it is important for parents and students to be aware of the school's test-taking policies and practices as well as how the test scores will be used. The right preparation will ensure that young people are able to put their best foot forward and meet with success.

SUGGESTIONS FOR STUDENTS

Students are heavily exposed to and impacted by all kinds of tests throughout their educational career. This is especially true today. Extensive research has been conducted on the effects of testing on students. This section is targeted toward students. It will provide valuable strategies for students to utilize to complete different kinds of tests and cope with numerous testing situations.

A student's first focus should be on preparing for a test. Students with better study skills and habits will score higher on tests. There are numerous ways to do this. Study, complete homework assignments, and review study materials on a regular basis. Study in a quiet, well-lit area free of distractions.

It is best to review material right after it is taught and still fresh in your memory. Begin reviewing the most important information first. Plan your time wisely so there is sufficient time to study for a test. Avoid cramming the night before a test. You will learn more by studying small amounts of information every day, and you are likely to retain the information over the long-term.

Attend review sessions when they are available to students. Listen for clues that a teacher or instructor may provide about a test. Take careful notes and ask questions about confusing material and the content that will be specified on the test; attempt to gather as much information as possible. Join a study group if one is available. Studying with peers who are serious about the test is helpful and makes preparing for a test more fun.

Train yourself to be an effective note-taker. Good notes are important when it comes to preparing well for a test. When a teacher writes something on a blackboard or overhead projector, write it down. Also, record ideas that a teacher repeats often. These are key points that will probably be covered in the test, so learn to recognize them.

Purchase notebooks and binders that allow you to organize notes in a flexible way by allowing you the freedom to move them around to suit your study needs.

Always record your own notes. Avoid relying on other students' notes whenever possible. You will learn better and achieve a better understanding from your own words. If you have a writing disability or a teacher who speaks quickly, consider purchasing a tape recorder to audiotape classes. You can take your time and transcribe what was said later. Remember that neat and legible notes are easier to study.

Be prepared for class by completing homework and required reading. You will get more out of the class when assigned work is corrected and discussed, and note-taking will be easier.

Make use of study guides, textbooks, class notes, and any other study materials provided by the teacher. Make your own study sheet by recording the main ideas and any other pertinent information you do not want to forget for the test. Consider organizing your notes using an outline format or graphic organizer that meets your needs. This will make it easier for you to retain key information.

Test yourself to determine your strong and weak areas. Continue to review areas that are strengths, but spend extra time rectifying your weaknesses.

Get a good night's sleep before the day of the test. Brains that have been robbed of sleep will not function well. Your memory recall will be much better if you have had enough restful sleep. Studies have shown that students who acquire adequate amounts of sleep perform better on tests than students who stay up all night cramming for a test.

Proper nutrition is also essential for students to perform well on tests. Eat a nutritious breakfast the morning of the test. Improved attention, quicker and more accurate retrieval of information, fewer errors, and better concentration will result. Whole grains and low protein are recommended. Avoid sugary foods that may make you feel overactive during the test.

Be sure to wake up early on the day of the test. This will allow you with enough time to eat breakfast and arrive at school on time. There is nothing more stressful than being late on the day of an important test and suffering from unnecessary test anxiety that could affect test performance. Bring an extra pen, pencil, calculator, scrap paper, or other items that may be helpful during the test and are allowed. If assigned seating is not required, choose a seat that is on the far left or right of the classroom to reduce the possibility of distraction.

Listen carefully to any instructions given before a test. Then read and follow the written directions that precede the test. Many students lose credit because they do not follow directions completely. Read through the test, and estimate how much time you will need to answer each item. Consider writing important facts, definitions, formulas, or key words you do not want to forget in the margin or on scrap paper.

Begin the actual test by answering the questions you know the answers to. Skip over difficult items, and go back to them later. Correctly answering the questions you know first helps to build confidence and reduce stress. Focus on the test, and try to refrain from letting your mind wander. If you become restless or nervous during the test, try wiggling your fingers and toes, taking a few deep breaths, or picturing yourself in a favorite relaxing place.

If you finish the test early, use the remaining minutes to check your answers over. Change only those answers you are sure are incorrect. Add details to items you feel require further information. Checking over the test will help you avoid careless errors or incomplete answers.

When you receive your test score or if the test is returned to you, take the opportunity to review the items you answered incorrectly. Ask the teacher for clarification of the score or an explanation as to why certain items were inaccurate. Frequently, a teacher will go over the test items along with an explanation of the answers. At that time, correct your errors, and take notes on what the teacher was asking for. This will prevent you from making the same mistakes in the future. If you are unhappy with your grade, ask the teacher if a makeup test is an option or if there are any other opportunities for you to improve your score.

Following these strategies before, during, and after taking a test should help most students reduce their test anxiety and improve their overall results. Students who do not have strong test-taking skills are at a disadvantage. Today's students are expected to take a variety of tests such as multiple-choice, true-false, oral, short answer, essay, quantitative math, and open book. They may be teacher-made or standardized. Critical reading and thinking skills are crucial for being successful on any test, yet, there are some specific strategies that can be used to tackle each type.

Try these strategies when completing multiple-choice tests:

- Read the test question before you look at answers.
- Determine the answer in your head before looking at the possible choices to avoid being swayed in the wrong direction by what is given.
- Read all of the choices given before selecting a final answer.
- Eliminate answers you know are incorrect to improve your odds of selecting the right one.
- Eliminate answers that are not grammatically linked to the question.
  - Correct answers are usually not written awkwardly or grammatically incorrect.
- Eliminate answers that are similar or use synonyms in them.
  - For example, if the choices are quick, large, fast, or wide, eliminate "quick" and "fast" because they are similar. "Large" and "wide" are more likely to be the ones to choose from.
- If you are completely unsure of the correct answer, make an educated guess.

- Refrain from continuously changing your mind because your first choice is usually the correct one unless you have misinterpreted the test item.
- If you are certain at least one of the choices is true, do not select "None of the above."
- If you are certain at least one of the choices is false, do not select "All of the above."
- If you are certain at least two of the choices are correct, recognize that "All of the above" is most likely the answer.
- Remember choices that are positively stated are more likely to be true than choices that are negatively stated.
- Recognize that the correct answer is typically the choice with the greatest amount of information.
- Be cautious of answers containing words like always, never, invariably, none, all, every, and must. Choose answers that contain valid wording and are less arguable.
  - This also holds true for true-false tests.
- Recognize that multiple-choice tests usually consist of questions or incomplete statements followed by a correct answer and four or five distracters or decoys. If the answers consist of a range of numbers, choose from the answers in the middle of the range if you do not know the correct answer. In test items with number ranges, remember that the decoys tend to be above and below the correct answer.
- Seek out answers that parallel each other.
  - Answers that contain wording such as "will speed a car up in cold weather" or "will slow a car down in cold weather" are examples of parallel responses that act as decoys in a multiple-choice test item.

These strategies may prove to be helpful when completing true and false tests.

- Recognize that you have a 50 percent chance of choosing the correct answer.
- Typically, remember that there are more true answers than false answers on the majority of tests.
  - This is especially true for teacher-made tests.
- Pay close attention to the qualifiers and key words as you read through each statement carefully.
- If you see qualifiers like never, always, and every, recognize that the statement must be true all of the time because these qualifiers point toward a false answer.
- If you see qualifiers like usually, sometime, and generally depending on the situation, recognize that the statement may be true or false because these qualifiers point toward a true answer.

- If any part of the statement is false, recognize that the entire statement is false.
- If part of the statement is true, recognize that it does not necessarily mean the entire statement is true.
- Do not overanalyze the statement. Instead, read it carefully, and determine what it is actually saying.

Draw from these strategies to complete short-answer tests:

- Prior to the test, make flash cards with test terminology. Write key terms, important dates, and concepts on the front. Write definitions, events, and explanations on the back.
- Pay attention to what the teacher or instructor emphasizes in class as well as information highlighted on study guides because you may be able to anticipate what will be asked on the test based on these clues.
- Attempt to answer all of the items. Try not to leave any of them blank. Even if you are unsure of yourself, write down your thoughts because you may be given partial credit.
- If you do not know an answer, skip over it, and go back to it after you complete the test. Make an educated guess.
  - Other test items may offer clues that will help you to generate an answer to the item you were initially unsure of.
- If you come up with more than one answer for a question, ask the teacher or instructor for clarification so you know what direction to move in.
- Read each question carefully to be sure you are answering it completely. Remember that some short-answer questions have multiple parts.
- When you have finished, go back and reread the questions and your answers to be sure your answers are accurate, worded properly, and free of grammatical errors.

When given a test using an essay format, try using these strategies:

- Begin by reading the directions so you will know how many of the essay questions you will actually need to answer.
  - Some tests will only require you to answer a specific amount of questions, like four out of five.
  - Other tests will require you to answer all of them.
- Read each essay question carefully to be sure you understand what you are being asked, then plan your answers accordingly. Include only pertinent information. Avoid providing excess information that is not relevant to the question. Instead, include plenty of facts and details that support your responses.

- Divide your time wisely among all of the questions. Avoid spending too much time on a single answer to a question.
- Create a brief outline before writing the actual response, resulting in a more organized essay.
- If a question requires factual information in the answer, refrain from including personal opinions.
- If you are required to write out your answers rather than type them, be sure your handwriting is neat and legible.
- Include introductory and concluding sentences, but focus on the portion of the essay that answers the question.
- If your essay contains several paragraphs, remember to include only one main idea per paragraph.
- If you are unsure about specific dates and time periods, use the word "approximately" with an estimated date or time.
- Try to answer all of the questions with at least some information.
  - Budgeting your time will help. If you have time at the end, you can go back and add additional information to incomplete answers.
- Use leftover time to reread your thoughts and edit your work for errors.

At times, you will be asked to take a test and allowed to use resources like a book or study materials to help you. Tests that allow such advantages are often more difficult, require answers that are scrutinized more, and graded more strictly. Consider these suggestions when confronted with an open book test:

- Familiarize yourself with the book and other relevant materials you will be allowed to use. Get a feel for where information is located.
- If you are permitted to bring a cheat sheet with you, include things like important concepts, key terms, definitions, important facts and details, and formulas on it, enabling you to search through the book less and save time.
- Highlight information, use Post-it notes or bookmarks, and write notes in the margins if allowed.
- Determine the easier questions first, and answer them. Choose questions that have answers you already know and will not require the use of the book.
- Use quotes to substantiate what you are saying, but be sure not to overlook your own thoughts and perceptions.

One final test you may have the opportunity to experience is an oral test. Some students with certain disabilities may be given oral tests. At times, teachers and instructors will prefer to use this method of testing with all students because it is the best way to assess the subject matter at hand. Regardless of the purpose, these hints may place you at a better advantage for taking this kind of test:

- Write the time and place of the test on a calendar or in a student planner.
  - Sometimes, oral tests are scheduled for students on an individual basis.
- Ask about the material you will be tested on. If the test is more like an oral presentation, ask if props or visuals that could enhance your presentation are permitted. If the test is more like an exam, envision the questions that will be asked. Prepare responses ahead of time.
- Practice what you will say on the day of the test in front of a mirror.
  - Audio and video taping are also helpful methods to evaluate body language, voice tone, and overall self-control.
- If you plan to use a computer on the day of an oral exam or presentation, be sure it is in good working order.
- Arrive early enough on the day of the test or presentation to set up or organize your thoughts, helping to make a good impression and reduce test anxiety.
- Be sure cell phones are turned off before an oral exam or presentation to avoid distracting interruptions.
- Dress appropriately to make a good impression during an oral exam. Dress in ways that will enhance your oral presentation, such as costuming.
- During an oral exam or presentation, maintain good eye contact and proper posture. Sit or stand up straight, and avoid slouching.
- Concentrate on the questions asked of you, and respond appropriately. If you do not understand the question, ask for clarification or the question to be repeated.
- Speak in complete sentences. If you become lost for words, begin your answer by restating the question to help provide you with a focus and the ability to remember information more quickly.
  - Memorizing and storing important pieces of information that you can draw from also helps.
- Remember that thanking a teacher or instructor at the end of the testing session is always a good idea, especially if the time period was scheduled just for you. Thank an audience for their attention at the end of an oral presentation.

There are no guarantees that these test-taking strategies will enable students to pass all of the tests they take. They should, however, improve their test-taking ability and promote critical thinking so it will be easier to make the best choices and improve overall test results.

Testing is a significant part of the educational process. It influences the decisions made about students' academic plans, and it is often a deciding factor when it comes to promotion. Students must also take an active role in their own education. Because test results influence so many aspects of students' academic careers and ultimately impacts their future, it is imperative to be well prepared with content and strategies that will lead to victory.

In order to promote academic achievement, parents must work with educators, stay involved in school activities, and ask questions that are necessary for their children's success. Strong partnerships must exist in all facets of education. Testing can make positive and negative contributions to children's lives. When parents, educators, and students are aware of what they can do to make a difference, positive results will prevail.

Chapter 3

What to Do if a Child Is Having a Problem in School

When a child is experiencing problems in school, it is important for the educators at the school and the parents to show an interest and send a message that they have not given up on him or her. Parents need to assume a role that is supportive, yet holds their child accountable for his or her success. Educators need to provide parents with the necessary information and appropriate venues to assume that role. It is important for parents to become aware of the signs of school failure as well as the solutions available to address them. Furthermore, parents must be willing to assist their child in finding solutions for his or her difficulties and failures.

Students often experience problems in four areas. One such area involves maintaining consistent daily attendance at school. Participating in courses that do not meet a student's needs and/or ability level is another area that can lead to problematic behavior. Poor effort and performance can occur when a child is not held accountable for his or her actions and school performance. Firm boundaries, consequences, and guidance are essential if a responsibility for learning is to develop. Finally, engaging in drug and alcohol abuse can contribute to a host of school-related problems.

In the past, educators were typically the ones who initiated contact with parents when a child was experiencing a problem in school. With an increase in school-related problems in today's society, it is now necessary for parents to share in this responsibility. Educators must encourage parents to make an appointment with their child's teachers or guidance counselor as a first step in searching for a solution when they detect that their child is experiencing some kind of difficulty.

This chapter was written with the parent in mind. It was designed to place some of the ownership on the parent of a child who is not meeting with success at school. It includes numerous strategies to address and solve the problematic areas faced by children today.

Information is also provided on children's learning styles. If a parent understands how his or her child learns best, that parent is in a more beneficial position to assist the child with schoolwork at home. If a parent's employment needs dictate an after-school program, information on what to look for in an effective after-school program is also outlined to assist a parent in selecting the most suitable one.

Although parents will tend to utilize this chapter more, educators will find the material useful and will be able to draw from many aspects when working with parents of problematic students.

PRACTICES FOR PARENTS

Indicators of School Problems or Failures

Many indicators exist to alert school-related problems or failures. Any of the following behaviors may indicate that your child is experiencing a problem at school:

- Failing grades
- Incomplete classwork or homework
- Changes in behavior, such as becoming withdrawn, aggressive, moody, or uncaring about school
- Changes in eating or sleeping habits
- An increase in notes sent home from your child's teachers
- A poor report card
- Loss of self-esteem or poor self-image
- Temper outbursts
- Poorly motivated in school
- Emotional highs and lows
- Excessive absenteeism
- Substance and tobacco use
- The desire to drop out of school

When any or several of these behaviors are evident, it is important to determine the source of the problem at hand and to find ways to help your child in dealing with it so he or she resume a path to school success. A number of suggestions and strategies have been found to be helpful in addressing and solving children's problems in school.

What to Do if Your Child Is Having a Problem in School

First of all, act quickly. Don't wait until the problem gets out of hand. It will only become more difficult to handle as time marches on. Talk with your child to grasp an understanding of where he or she is coming from. Remain calm throughout the dialogue. Ask questions and listen quietly for clues that might point to the source or contribute to a better understanding of the trouble.

Next, contact and talk with the people involved. Begin with teachers if your child's problem is academic. Usually, teachers will see things from a different point of view. Politely listen to their side and then explain your views. Ask your child to do the same. Focus on discovering a solution, not assigning blame.

If you, your child, and the teacher cannot find a solution, meet with the school principal. Principals have a wealth of experience in dealing with student problems and may offer a solution that can work. Again, a calm and courteous approach works best.

If your child's difficulties stem from academic and behavioral issues, seek out the child's guidance counselor. Guidance counselors are typically equipped to advise parents in both the academic and behavioral realms. Many schools prefer parents contact guidance counselors as a first step. It may be the counselor's responsibility to organize a meeting among interested parties. Schools often provide handbooks at the start of the school year outlining the course of action for parents to follow to address numerous concerns.

Parents are encouraged to get in touch with the school anytime they have a question, a comment, or a concern. There are four specific times, however, when a parent should make contact:

- If you see a drop in your child's grades
- If you see a dramatic change in your child's behavior
- If you suspect that your child may not be telling the truth about an incident or situation
- If there is a change in your family, including a new marriage, divorce, serious illness, death, birth of a child, or any other change that may affect family dynamics

It is important to remember that both the parents and the school staff want what is best for a child. By working together, problems can be solved.

Be involved in your child's education. Research continues to tell us that children are more successful when their parents take an active interest in their education. There are a number of ways to achieve this:

- Learn when report cards will be distributed and carefully review it with your child when you receive it. A report card discussion should act more

like a positive learning experience rather than as a negative experience that
can cause conflict in the home.

- Remember that praise and encouragement go a long way. Focus on your
  child's talents and strengths. Acknowledge and celebrate your child's successes whenever possible.
- Learn when the school will hold parent conferences and special parent
  nights. Be mindful of the dates and times, and make a commitment to
  attend as many events as possible. This conveys a strong positive message
  to your child that you care.
- Schools provide a host of information for parents to read throughout the
  school year, so read parent newsletters and all other types of literature sent
  home by the school. Ask your child if he or she has any school-to-home
  communications to share with you on a daily basis.
- Take the time to research school supports that may be available to assist
  your child not only during the school day, but also after school. Many
  schools provide after-school tutoring programs and homework clubs. Take
  advantage of these resources if your child qualifies.
- Talk with your child about the benefits of education and the positive effects
  it will have on his or her future. Children need to know that you, as a parent, value education. They need to recognize that a strong correlation exists
  between school success and the ability to succeed in life.

After-School Programs

If your child's school does not offer an after-school program, seek out organizations in the community that may provide one. Refer to the school, the
newspaper, bulletin board flyers in stores where you shop, the library, the
church, or social service agencies. Research the days and hours that children
may attend as well as the cost factor. Ask about transportation requirements
to and from the facility.

The following list includes the qualities parents should look for when
selecting an effective after-school program. It provides parents with the
information needed to choose a program that is suitable for their child and
satisfies their own desires and scheduling needs. An effective after-school
program:

- Recognizes and promotes the self-worth of each child who attends
- Recognizes the individual differences and cultural diversity of the children
  who participate
- Provides academic support, assistance with homework, tutoring, and other
  learning activities

- Provides enrichment opportunities to add to a child's learning in school, especially those that deal with thinking and problem-solving skills
- Provides recreational activities that support a child's physical development
- Provides age-appropriate information about careers and career training options
- Employs responsible and caring adults
- Employs adults who are trained to assist with academics and offers social, emotional, and physical support
- Provides a safe and clean environment
- Provides nutritious snacks and meals, if appropriate
- Houses good academic resources and sports equipment
- Provides quiet study space

Learning Styles

Educators receive training and academic preparation in the area of children's learning styles. It is equally important for parents to be aware of the ways in which children learn. Children have ways in which they learn best.

Three common learning styles exist: visual, auditory, and physical learning. By identifying the style that your child learns best with, you will be better able to offer assistance that promotes positive and successful learning experiences. Your child's teachers can help you to determine the learning style unique to your child. These learning styles are outlined below, along with some helpful strategies that can be used at home.

Visual learners learn best by watching and observing. They look for clues that will help them to form pictures of the material in their heads.

- Make flash cards with information that needs to be memorized for a test, project, or assignment.
- Draw symbols or pictures to help with understanding.
- Highlight key words, phrases, pictures, charts, diagrams, and so forth to help with understanding.
- Make charts to organize information.
  - Your child's teachers may have some ideas for other kinds of graphic organizers that can be used to organize and simplify information.
- Make lists, or use notes or use an assignment pad to write down upcoming tests, projects, or assignments that should not be forgotten.

Auditory learners learn best by hearing information presented verbally.

- Read aloud together.
- Encourage your child to read aloud when he or she studies so he or she can hear the information.
- Talk about solutions to problems together.
- Tell stories together.
- Play word games together. Try to incorporate school study material.
- Have your child make use of a tape recorder when studying.

Physical learners learn best through movement (touch, feel, and experience). They often enjoy discovering how things work. Physical learners like to try things out by handling them. They prefer to show you rather than tell you about something.

- Encourage your child to get involved in science or math laboratories at school.
- Encourage your child to participate in a drama group.
- Request that your child display his or her learning through presentations at school.
- Request that your child make models to demonstrate learning at school.
- Encourage your child to take notes and draw diagrams for new study material.

Recognizing and understanding learning styles will place parents in a better position to work with their child, their child's teachers, and any other school personnel when solving problems and creating positive situations that lead to student success.

Useful Parent Internet Sites

This chapter touched upon some of the indicators of behaviors that can lead to school failure as well as some of the actions that parents could take to work with the school to ultimately improve a troublesome situation. In addition to the information provided in this chapter, parents should be aware that numerous websites exist that can be utilized to gather additional information and resources regarding parental involvement when a child experiences some type of school failure.

It is suggested that parents investigate sites that act as information networks, offer assistance with homework and study habits, offer help in dealing with parental issues, provide information on parental involvement in education, and enlighten parents with methods to deal with children and youth with disabilities. Parents are encouraged to take advantage of the Internet whenever possible and to use it as a tool to broaden their knowledge about ways to increase the positive development and successful education of their children.

When a child experiences some type of school failure, it affects many. The child suffers, the school environment is disrupted, and the parent is frustrated with feelings of helplessness. This can change when schools and families work together to find solutions. When parents feel empowered, they are more likely to become engaged in their child's education, and partnerships between schools and families can emerge and grow.

Chapter 4

Mentoring

The concept of mentoring has long existed in the business world. In recent years, it has extended to the field of education. Mentoring is a partnership that involves dialogue between those involved and results in reflection, action, and learning. A mentorship refers to a developmental relationship between two people, one of whom is more knowledgeable in one or more areas. This individual typically helps the other by sharing knowledge, community resources, and psychosocial support.

Mentoring has historical roots. Mentorships stem from segments of Greek history, and formal and informal mentorships are recognized in Homer's *Odyssey*. The mentors were older and wiser masters who guided young and aspiring apprentices. Other situations involved patrons who directed and shaped their protégés. These kinds of mentorships are still in practice within the religions of Hinduism and Buddhism. These mentorships often involve elders who supervise younger people and guide them in academic and life situations.

Programs have been developed for youths to help them in a variety of ways. Many of these programs target the academic, social, and psychological needs of young people. Today, there is a growing need to reach a much larger population than ever before. Mentoring has achieved extensive public recognition due to its extraordinary success. Research reveals improvement in academic achievement, school attendance, and relationships with parents and peers.

The purpose of this chapter is to identify the forms of mentoring that are most appropriate to use with young people today within academic institutions. Information will be provided to assist educators in setting up a mentoring program to serve their students. The chapter will also reach out to parents to teach them the benefits of mentoring and encourage them to serve as mentors to their children and teens.

ESSENTIALS FOR EDUCATORS

The research on mentoring has produced encouraging findings, yet problems still exist concerning many aspects of mentoring programs. Many young people are in need of mentoring programs. Traditional models have not been able to accommodate all who could benefit from participating. Mentors are scarce. Funding is inadequate. Programs often rely, to some degree, on parent referrals, and many parents are unaware of the eligibility criteria or the gains from participating in them. Educators have much work to do to incur financial support, recruit mentors, and publicize programs.

In many secondary and postsecondary schools, mentoring programs or mentorships are offered to support program completion, build self-confidence, and encourage the mentee to further his or her education or take the necessary steps to advance in the workplace.

Today, mentoring programs and mentorships are becoming more popular in elementary schools. Mentors at this level not only support academics, but also become involved in the lives of children to help them cope with difficult situations. They generally form a bond with children that extends beyond the educational level. Mentors often encourage mentees to discuss various problems in their lives. They very often become surrogate adults who offer advice, compassion, and understanding.

Mentoring programs and mentorships can serve any segment of the educational population. Such support can extend beyond the elementary school student who is having difficulty in a subject area or an at-risk high school student. Gifted students can benefit from receiving some mentoring in a subject they excel in and wish to take that knowledge to a higher level. With the assistance of a mentor, language minority students can become more proficient in the English language, academic subjects in the curriculum, and social skills.

Students with low self-esteem, behavioral issues, or social interaction can profit from a relationship with a mentor. Academics do not have to be the central focus of a mentorship. Mentors are in a unique position to recognize difficulties that students are experiencing both in and out of the classroom and can make teachers and parents aware of such problems.

Very often, students from single-parent or low-income homes endure extraordinary experiences that greatly impact their lives both in and out of school. Providing these students with a mentoring experience can offer compassion, understanding, and coping skills. A mentor is often in a pivotal place to discover situations within a family unit that could be rectified by acquiring assistance from a community agency, for example, for the family.

Mentoring programs and mentorships aid students in other ways. When students receive recognition and attention from a mentor, it tends to boost their self-esteem. They have the desire to attend school more often and become aware of the value of an education. Schools also reap the benefits of mentoring. Schools that offer mentoring programs and mentorships have a lower dropout rate, and more students further their education. The image of a school is heightened when businesses become involved in the mentoring process by providing mentors or funding, and more people ultimately become involved in the educational process.

Mentoring can take on many forms: formal, informal, peer mentoring, reverse mentoring, cascading mentoring, group mentoring, mentoring round tables, mentoring circles, and mastermind mentoring. Some of these approaches lend themselves better to school settings than others do.

Arranged relationships are considered formal. Formal mentorships are typically arranged through community or educational agencies that seek to match people who are likely to connect with each other in positive ways. Mentors are selected based on their experience, knowledge, skills, and ability to share the knowledge they possess. Some formal mentoring programs are values-oriented; some are career-oriented. Because a third-party establishes formal mentoring relationships, they are often viewed as being the best managed.

A formal mentoring program is structured, and a clear framework is created. Expectations and goals are established, and a process to achieve them is outlined. The program also dictates ground rules and timeframes.

Informal mentoring just happens. Two people discover they are compatible and get together periodically to share ideas. One assumes the role of the teacher or mentor; the other assumes the role of the student or mentee. Together, they engage in conversation that produces insight. The conversation does not have to follow a particular course or format. The mentee intuitively chooses an individual to serve as a mentor who will fulfill roles such as advisor, coach, or advocate. Both parties agree to the mentoring.

Several types of formal and informal mentoring program models can be chosen to implement, including the friendship model, the nurturing model, and the apprenticeship model.

The friendship model is more like peer mentoring where there is little hierarchy. Because the mentorship is a partnership between peers who usually take turns mentoring each other, this method of mentoring must be strictly monitored by an adult or professional to ensure that true mentoring is taking place.

The nurturing model is usually used to establish a relationship between an adult and an elementary school student. Very often, this relationship incorporates more than just the academic realm. Students at this level frequently need nurturing. Mentors work with students who are deprived in some way at home or are abused and need an adult companion to help them cope with or overcome obstacles that keep them from growing academically or emotionally. These students lack the nurturing that most children take for granted. Therefore, these mentors must be prepared to handle issues greater than the academics.

An apprenticeship model helps students to get the education they need for a career they want without going to college. The mentor personally guides the student's education primarily through experiences he or she arranges, as well as through specific course manual work augmenting the hands-on lessons. The training is individualized and flexible. A mentor skilled in a field is chosen. He or she then offers an unpaid apprenticeship to a student. Students who apply to a program using an apprenticeship model are interviewed to ensure they are committed, focused, and competent. The mentor also assists students in finding a job when they appear ready for employment.

Although it is not always necessary, a strong bond between the mentor and the mentee can facilitate the process and make it more effective. This holds true more in situations involving informal mentoring than in formal mentoring programs.

Historically, mentoring has involved a one-on-one relationship with informal and unstructured interaction. Modern forms of mentoring encompass more structured approaches.

With peer mentoring, two colleagues or peers mentor each other. In the business world, executives are mentored by nonexecutives. Each level of an organization mentors those below it with cascading mentoring. Group mentoring involves one mentor who mentors several individuals in a group setting. Mentoring circles also meet in a group setting, but each participant mentors one person and is mentored by another. Peers interact in a group mentoring discussion in mentoring round tables. Finally, mastermind mentoring and business coaching involve experts who coach novices.

Peer mentoring is a form of mentoring that can take place in a school setting. Peer mentoring can be effective because people of the same age with similar experiences come together to discuss comparable issues or situations. It is a good way for the mentor to practice educational and social skills while helping the mentee to receive academic remediation and to adapt to new situations.

Peer mentors are usually selected for their sensitive attitudes toward others, self-confidence, social skills, and reliability. Reliability is important for mentees to feel confident that the mentor will be available during positive and negative circumstances.

Peer mentoring mainly happens in secondary schools and is useful for students transitioning from one educational setting to another, such as from middle school to high school. The benefits gained from peer mentoring have caused it to filter down to the elementary level.

The amount of time that peer mentors and mentees meet varies, depending upon the educational or social situation. At the elementary level, peer mentoring is useful to new students who are in need of an immediate friend to acclimate them to the school. Elementary-level students may meet with their peer mentor several times during the week if the mentee is experiencing academic issues. Usually, the mentor and the mentee communicate using a person-to-person format.

At the secondary level, peer mentors may meet with their mentees as often as once each week or as little as three or four times each month, depending on the issue at hand. Higher levels of communication can be used, such as e-mailing, telephoning, or texting. As with any form of mentoring, peer mentoring should be well-defined, measureable, monitored, and assessed by a trained professional.

Group mentoring is another form of mentoring that schools can utilized. In fact, a school is the most common setting. It is becoming more popular, in part, because it involves fewer obstacles associated with one-on-one mentoring. It also broadens the range of mentors because it attracts individuals who prefer a group setting and are less likely to volunteer for one-on-one mentoring. It is also less costly than traditional forms of mentoring.

Typically, mentoring groups can have as many as 32 participants; however, most groups are comprised of approximately 10 individuals. Their average meeting time is 21 hours per month. Group members engage in both structured and unstructured activities, and their focus varies. Topics for discussion may include academics, homework, sports, socialization, health, community service, team building, leadership development, the arts, and cultural diversity. Group mentoring programs are more likely to involve youth from ethnic and racial minority groups, but they can be successful with a broad spectrum of individuals.

Group mentoring greatly enhances social skills and the participants' ability to work with peers in a group. Improvements in relationships can also be seen. The quality of the mentor-mentee relationships varies widely and depends on the group's focus and activities.

Central to the concept of mentoring is conversation. The conversation piece assists mentees in reflecting upon their own experiences, making knowledgeable decisions, and acting appropriately on the ideas that are discussed. Goal-setting and problem-solving are two other important skills that can be accomplished through meaningful conversation with a mentor.

Regardless of the approach used, the function of a mentor is to establish a relationship with the mentee, pose relevant questions, and tap into the mentee's repertoire of knowledge. Today's mentor does not have to be an older and wiser individual, as in the past. A mentor is someone a mentee can learn from, regardless of age or status. Today's mentor needs to be skilled in leading a mentoring conversation.

Through a mentoring conversation, mentees are expected to reflect upon their own experiences and issues at hand. They gather information from numerous sources that could be used to solve problems. They sort through options, develop a plan of action, and put the plan into practice. Part of the learning experience for mentees involves continuous review of the plan and its outcome.

Effective mentoring conversation enhances a mentee's thinking process, especially if the mentor utilizes skilled questioning techniques. It is through careful questioning that a mentee becomes more independent and relies less on the mentor for answers. An important goal of the mentoring relationship is for the mentee to develop critical thinking skills to improve decision-making, weigh consequences, and ultimately take responsibility for actions and behavior.

Establishing a mentoring program for students involves careful planning. Educational mentoring programs are designed to support young people who are disadvantaged in some way. Begin the design of the program by establishing objectives and guidelines for more than just program content. Some school districts set up a mentoring committee composed of staff members and knowledgeable professionals in the field to oversee the design and implementation. The committee is also responsible for developing a process to select mentors and mentees.

It is important for a committee to examine the needs of the school and the student population. It is also important for the members to identify the school problems and the student problems that require the most help. This information is crucial to enable a mentoring program to include essential components to address the most significant needs.

Once a program is in place, selecting a program coordinator to facilitate the program will allow it to operate more smoothly. A program coordinator can serve as a manager, contact person, and recruiter. A program coordinator can also use the criteria developed by the mentoring committee to select and pair mentors with mentees, establish a schedule for the participants, monitor and support the program, and evaluate its success.

An infrastructure constructed to meet school, student, and staff needs will contribute to the success of a mentoring program. Within a strong program structure are individuals leading the effort with energy, skills, time, and a sense of commitment. Volunteers are useful to a mentoring program. A successful mentoring program, however, cannot depend solely on the work of volunteers. Volunteers who are not committed to the program or burn out emotionally tend to leave and pursue other interests.

Discussion regarding the logistics of the program should take place. The outcome should reveal where, when, and how often mentors and mentees should meet. Because it often takes six months for mentors and mentees to form close relationships, it is recommended that the two meet once a week for one hour for an academic year.

It is also suggested that students meet with their mentors on school grounds under the supervision of certified staff members if the mentors are not part of the faculty or credentialed professionals. This is a good way to avoid liability issues. If students will be meeting with their mentors at an off-school site, insurance and liability issues should be addressed before mentoring sessions begin.

Before a mentoring program can commence, monetary issues must be resolved so the program does not dissolve midstream. Identify sources of income. It is hoped that the school district will recognize the value of such a program and contribute school budget funds. Grants are a good source to tap into for revenue. Community groups and businesses may be willing to make monetary contributions. To receive the most dollars for this initiative, it is a good idea to make the plan attractive so possible contributors will conclude that the program will be beneficial and successful.

Criteria for selecting mentors and mentees are an integral part of any mentoring program. Decide on what type of student the program will target. Invite teachers and counselors to furnish names of students who fit the profile as possible candidates. Interview the students. Once candidates are selected, meet with parents and mentees to explain the program. Goals, structure, and expectations should be discussed. Parents and mentees should have the opportunity to ask questions to make them feel as comfortable as possible.

Students who are unlikely to benefit from the program should not be considered for acceptance. Successful mentoring relationships will not form for students who are reluctant to make a commitment or if their demeanor demonstrates an unwillingness to participate.

Be certain that parents are willing to cooperate and support the mentors' lessons at home. Inform them that they are responsible for transportation to and from mentoring sessions unless other arrangements are appropriate. Some districts require parents to sign contracts to further ensure their participation and commitment to the program.

Recruiting mentors can be challenging. Be cognizant of the qualities a mentor should possess. Determine the expectations they are expected to fulfill. Communicate the large time commitment involved. Seek out mentors who will commit to the program for at least one year.

Decide if the mentors will be chosen from the school, community, or both venues. It is advantageous to a program to recruit mentors from a variety of backgrounds such as educators, older students, businesspeople, church members, and community activists. Solicit mentors from the community by advertising in newspapers, church bulletins, or flyers that can be sent to community organizations and businesses. Purchase radio or television time if affordable.

Directly speaking to community organizations is also effective. Testimonials from mentors and mentees can further reinforce the intent of a mentoring program. When recruiting, it is helpful to communicate success stories.

All potential participants must be carefully screened. A background check on all potential mentors must be administered. Their backgrounds must be studied, and their interests and intentions must be carefully scrutinized. Require applicants to provide information regarding their experience working with young people. Ask them to reveal their motivation to become a mentor and the age group and subjects they feel comfortable interacting with.

Hold informational meetings for prospective mentors to outline the logistics, goals, and objectives of the program. Choose mentors who have good communication and interpersonal skills. Seek out individuals who appear committed to their mentees. Mentors who lack dedication to their mentorship can do more harm than good.

When it becomes evident that a mentor is not fulfilling his or her obligations, especially if it is early in the relationship, ask the individual to reconsider his or her decision to be a mentor. Suggest that another form of volunteer work may be more suitable. Make every effort to obtain another mentor for the mentee as soon as possible.

To avoid harmful situations, train mentors. Inform them about what to expect from mentees, and advise them on how to respond to various situations. Provide them with basic information on the development of children and teens, how various age groups learn and communicate, and the challenges that each age group presents. Cultural diversity training can also be helpful in certain educational settings.

Mentors should be trained by experienced educational professionals. Mentoring goals and objectives should be explained well. Strategies for developing meaningful and effective mentoring relationships should be provided. Building trust between mentors and mentees is absolutely necessary, and methods for constructing trusting relationships must be offered to prospective mentors. Different styles of communication can complement relationship-building and should be pursued during training.

In order for a mentorship to be successful, the pairing of mentors with mentees should be carefully considered and monitored. The individual needs of the mentee are first and foremost. Mentors are encouraged to be conscious of them and plan activities and sessions according to the mentee's interests and goals.

Common interests between mentors and mentees are also important to keep in mind when establishing mentorships. These interests can extend beyond the academic domain and include hobbies and leisure time activities.

Scheduled meeting times should take place on a regular basis. It is helpful if the mentor and mentee live in close proximity to the school so the school can easily schedule the meeting times to accommodate both parties.

Race and gender are not imperative to the mentoring process. It has been noted, however, that parents are more comfortable with same race or gender matches. It has been found that gender matches have more of a positive effect than race matches do. Gender matches tend to enhance the relationship due to factors such as common interests.

School districts that wish to establish a mentoring program and require assistance are advised to consider the mentoring resources offered by Ann Rolfe, founder and director of Mentoring Works. For the last 15 years, Dr. Rolfe has helped organizations, institutions of learning, and individuals benefit from mentoring. Her website alone provides comprehensive information about the many facets of mentoring as well as a host of ideas school districts can draw from to establish a suitable mentoring program that fulfills their needs. Workshops and ongoing support are also available and tailored to create and maintain an effective mentoring program.

Research reveals that students who are at a disadvantage are more successful educationally, socially, and emotionally when they are involved in a relationship with a mentor. Typically, mentoring relationships are established within the school setting with the help of educators and professionals. It has also been found that any student can benefit by a relationship with another individual who offers unconditional understanding and support. Such relationships can occur in a school setting, and they can extend beyond it.

Individuals who come from a variety of backgrounds serve as mentors for our youth. Educators, professionals in the field, or trained volunteers from business and the community are likely choices. But we cannot overlook yet one more possibility. A parent can also fulfill the role of a mentor.

PRACTICES FOR PARENTS

Research tells us that mentoring has more positive effects on the behavior of youths than other methods. Young people involved in mentorships are less likely to engage in drug use or alcohol abuse. They attend school more regularly, skip classes less frequently, raise the goals and expectations they have for themselves, and improve their grades. Mentored students are less disruptive in class and experience healthier relationships with adults and peers.

Until recently, formal mentoring programs usually provided mentoring services and arranged the mentorships. Today's parents are stepping into the role of mentor and really making a difference. They have the advantage of positively influencing their children and teens before they become at risk for failure by providing them with confidence, coping skills, and strong decision-making ability.

Parents are their children's first teachers. This familiar phrase reminds us of the impact parents have on their children's development physically, emotionally, socially, and, at times, academically. They do this through mentoring in a sense. Parents really begin mentoring their children from the time they are born. They begin the process by teaching their children necessary basic skills like walking, talking, eating, and dressing themselves.

As a child grows, mentoring increases to include teaching concepts like letter and number recognition that will prepare them for success in school. Later, parents mentor their children by reinforcing what they are taught in school at home.

Mentoring groups with other children in the neighborhood can form. Children can be taught to communicate, play, and interact with each other. Families can share in educational goals. Parents can teach their children everyday skills that can be used in their neighborhood and beyond. Reading street signs, shopping together, and planning meals and family events together are a few of the skills that can be developed.

As children become older, mentoring takes a different focus. Situations arise that require critical thinking and sound decision-making ability. Parents are called upon to not only act as strong role models, but also as mentors who can provide skills to keep their children and teens safe. Parents should continue to serve as mentors by reinforcing what transpires at school at a higher level. Parents can call upon teachers for suggestions to help their youngsters with problem areas and to support academic areas their youngsters excel in.

Structured mentoring sessions should take place in quiet areas of the home every day. The sessions do not have to be dull and uninteresting. They can involve games devised by the parent, along with the child or teen.

Parents who mentor recognize and acknowledge that their children and teens have an identity shaped by their interests, strengths, and talents. Between the ages of nine and seventeen, a young person's identity emerges.

Parents with a willingness to mentor abandon an autocratic parenting style. They replace control with respect. They display love and acceptance during situations involving pain, anger, and fear. They focus on positive behaviors, are nonjudgmental, and respond well in stressful situations. They respect the path their children and teens choose to follow in life.

Susan G. Weinberger, author of *The Mentor Handbook*, developed the following guidelines for parents who wish to mentor their children and teens. The suggestions are useful and practical. If practiced consistently, the results will be rewarding.

- Give special attention to positive actions and behaviors.
- Be nonjudgmental.
- Maintain control, and respond appropriately in stressful situations.
- Show tolerance in frustrating situations.
- Be a strong role model by avoiding alcohol or drug abuse.
- Be an active listener.
- Talk to your child or teen on his or her level.
- Provide guidance and leadership.
- Respect alternative lifestyles.
- Be on time for events and activities with your child or teen.
- Show consideration for your youngster's dignity.
- Be a responsible parent.
- Celebrate accomplishments.
- Delegate adult responsibilities only when your child or teen can handle them.

It is suggested that parents break the bonds of dependency and begin mentoring early on, that is, when their children enroll in school on a full-time basis, as opposed to waiting until the teenage years. Mentoring parents are not the only influence on their children and teens. Mentoring parents believe in building a supportive network for them. Tapping into community resources and sports teams provides additional positive role models who nurture and support growing individuals.

Teen years are especially difficult. These young people are exposed to and move through a variety of situations at record speed. Change is constant and guidance is crucial. Parents may find themselves in different roles from listener to coach to advisor. Communication is key to knowing what their adolescents are thinking, feeling, and doing. Non-mentoring parents tend to react and dictate how their teen should respond to a situation. Mentoring parents tend to offer unconditional love and propose nonjudgmental suggestions that will, in turn, build trust.

Some parents may feel they are too busy or unable to effectively mentor their children, but believe their children would benefit by mentorships.

In situations like these, parents are encouraged to enroll in a parent-mentor training program if one is accessible or to contact the school district for mentoring programs that are available.

Parent-mentor training programs are known to teach parents the skills they need to effectively mentor their children and adolescents. Such programs have been tested and assessed at Boulder High School and Baseline Middle School in Boulder, Colorado, after the horrific Columbine High School massacre.

The programs target grades five through twelve and are available to parents nationwide through participating school districts. In four two-hour sessions, parents learn how to be a mentor to their own children and teens using techniques found in *The Parent-Mentors Guidebook* by Alexia Parks and Steve Anderson. Along with this guide, they co-developed parent-mentor training programs for school districts. The guidebook functions like a workbook with mentoring exercises to teach young people how to make positive choices that guide them through their at-risk years. The guidebook and training programs have won popularity with parents.

Parents are encouraged to study the possible choices to be sure the best mentoring program is selected for their child or teen. Once selected, make every effort to know the workings of the program. Meet and get to know the coordinator, the professional staff, the mentors, and the mentees involved. If the mentoring sessions will not be held in a school, ensure that the facility is a safe environment conducive to helping your youngster.

Once parents are comfortable with the staff and structure, they must decide if the program is suitable and will benefit their child or teen. Ask about the success rate, especially for low-performing or at-risk participants. When your youngster enters into a program:

- Setup an appointment with the assigned mentor, and ask about the assessments that will be used to determine the course of action.
- Preview the lesson plans that will be used, and request copies to be prepared to offer support at home.
- Make a commitment to be responsible for bringing your youngster to and from the sessions.

It is important for parents to sign on with enthusiasm for the program. Hopefully, a bond will form between the mentor and the mentee, resulting in positive outcomes. If at any time a parent is not satisfied with the arrangement or the experience, he or she should contact the program coordinator immediately. In fact, consistent communication among those involved is essential for the success of the mentorship and the success of the mentoring program.

Parents require additional parenting skills to deal with the challenges their children and adolescents face in the twenty-first century. Today's parents need conflict resolution skills, acceptance skills, and mentoring skills. When parents mentor their own children and teens or enroll them in an effective mentoring program, they will respond with trust, honesty, and confidence at home, in school, and in the community.

The effectiveness of any mentoring program is dependent upon meeting student needs; obtaining administrative backing; attaining parental support; and finding time, manpower, and resources to make it work. School districts are advised to take ample time to organize, develop, and implement the program. They must generate enough monetary and human resources to support the program.

Educators must be open and honest with parents and students concerning participation, and every effort must be made to match mentors and mentees in compatible mentorships. Parents must be responsible for bringing their children and teens to mentoring sessions, staying involved in what transpires, and supporting what happens in sessions at home. Students must be committed and tap into their potential to become better students and people. They also need to be given a vehicle to give their input into the program and the mentorship. They need opportunities to voice their concerns along with their positive experiences.

Mentoring relationships can develop into nurturing relationships that last a lifetime. Mentoring programs that are established by partnerships among educators, parents, and students breed successful mentorships that help young people improve as students, human beings, and contributing members of the community. Successful mentorships ultimately raise self-esteem and provide young people with the skills they need to be successful in life.

Chapter 5

How to Encourage Reading

Children benefit most from reading instruction when they come to school already interested in books and are proficient in reading at their grade level. This is not always the case, and educators are faced with the challenges of motivating students to develop a love for books and correcting reading deficiencies so their students will acquire sufficient understanding of the material they read. Neither task is easy. Parents who provide meaningful and pleasurable reading experiences are helping children to learn the joy of reading as well as supporting the skills taught in classrooms. Yet, many parents may be unaware of how important a role they can play in reading development.

This chapter summarizes the current body of relevant reading research for today's educators and provides information on the best practices for educators to draw from to provide their students with experiences that will enhance their reading ability and their interest in books.

This chapter is also designed to assist parents with the tools they will need in order to select appropriate books for children. Books have a strong influence on the mind and should be selected thoughtfully and carefully. Suggestions are provided that will encourage good reading habits both in and out of the home.

The skill of reading is key for students to understand and connect to the world around them. Developing and improving this skill results in better readers and can be accomplished more effectively when parents and educators have the same focus and work together.

ESSENTIALS FOR EDUCATORS

Reading is considered a necessary skill for survival, and failure to read during the years spent in elementary school reduces an individual's likelihood for success in school and later in life.

At the core of many reading programs is a set of reading readiness skills that students at a variety of grade levels lack. A host of reading programs exist that promise to address the needs of students deficient in reading and to raise overall student achievement in the area of reading. It is understandable why teachers have such a difficult time choosing one for their students. While many of these reading programs claim to be built on evidence-based research, it is important to remember that effective programs should emphasize good literature, reading for enjoyment, and meaningful content.

Good reading programs are based on sound evidence resulting from studies on their effectiveness and success; however, many teachers have not been trained in interpreting research that is valid and invalid. To obtain the most valid research, choose evidence written by the researcher who actually conducted the study. Teachers themselves possess their own research that comes from the many years they have spent teaching reading in the classroom. While evidence-based practices are important, a teacher's ability to assess students' needs is equally important to determine the strategies from the appropriate reading program to best address deficiencies.

To determine how effective a program is for students, it is crucial to monitor student learning and skill maintenance on a continuous basis. Students should be required to respond during instruction, and a schedule to assess reading progress should be determined with low-performing students to be assessed more frequently. When a teacher observes that little or no progress has been made after several weeks, a new instructional strategy should be chosen.

A child's failure to read by the age of nine is a strong predictor of adult illiteracy. Reading difficulty and reading failure are particularly critical in schools that serve minority students and students who come from economically disadvantaged households. These students are less likely to speak Standard English. These students are also less likely to enter kindergarten with the necessary preliteracy experiences needed for early learning.

In addition, greater than 50 percent of urban learners and nearly 70 percent of African American and Hispanic learners are deficient in reading.

These alarming conclusions indicate that reading interventions must be applied early in a child's educational career. For older students who are identified as lacking in reading proficiency, reading interventions must target weaknesses, build on strengths, and be relevant and meaningful to the student. Reading programs should offer consistency and duration of instruction. Interventions that develop or improve decoding, word knowledge, oral reading, and comprehension are necessary for proficient reading.

When selecting appropriate reading strategies to apply, teachers are encouraged to connect them with each student's culture, ethnicity, and personal experience as often as possible. Materials that incorporate multicultural literature are strongly recommended for minority students to make meaningful connections and increase understanding.

The National Reading Panel advocates a balanced reading approach for young children to alleviate reading gaps and address reading deficiencies. Their practical approach suggests that phonemic awareness, alphabet understanding, and automaticity of the code form the basis for beginning reading instruction. Further, good reading instruction is explicit, intensive, and systematic.

The term "explicit" refers to targeting specific reading skills. "Intensive" suggests providing more learning opportunities that involve increased repetition of reading skills already learned. "Systematic" indicates sequential skill building.

Likewise, the National Early Literacy Panel generated a useful list of skills and abilities for young children that may serve as indicators of success in the areas of reading and writing, including alphabet knowledge, print knowledge, environmental print, invented spelling, listening comprehension, oral language and vocabulary, phonemic awareness, phonological short-term memory, rapid naming, visual memory, and visual perceptual skills.

Young children need opportunities to connect oral language to literacy by interacting with adults and peers. Singing and making music, responding to stories, participating in discussions, and listening for specific purposes are recommended.

Provide young children with opportunities to have fun with letters to improve alphabet knowledge and phonemic awareness. Letter and sound games, alphabet puzzles and books, and rhyming and language games are beneficial.

Young children also require opportunities to make sense of print. To help achieve this, model writing while stating the words aloud, write down children's contributions during discussions, utilize the printed content in books, and demonstrate how to track print from left to right when reading.

Another startling statistic present in the research on reading is that the vocabulary that a young child possesses when entering first grade not only predicts his or her word reading ability, but also predicts his or her eleventh-grade comprehension ability.

Instruction in vocabulary knowledge that extends beyond just using words in contextual situations works well. Frequent exposure to words in a variety of contexts is necessary so young children can discover the many dimensions of words. To achieve this, teachers can identify important words within the content they are teaching that can extend into many situations and generate examples to show this. Provide occasions for students to hear these words again, and encourage students to identify new words in different situations that relate to the original vocabulary words. These discoveries add to some very positive growth in vocabulary.

Research tells us that students who are successful readers learn to read words using four different means: contextual guessing, letter-sound decoding, analogy, and sight. Possessing a sound and extensive vocabulary enhances reading comprehension and improves a child's ability to become an active participant in society. Here is where teachers, schools, and parents can make a difference.

A school's language arts curriculum should provide extensive oral language experiences in which students are not only exposed to rich vocabulary but also have opportunities to share the meaningful vocabulary they encounter from their own reading, conversations with others, television and other media sources, and day-to-day experiences.

Teachers know that books are a wonderful source for building a rich vocabulary, and students should be encouraged to read on a daily basis. Classrooms need to house libraries with a variety of literature to meet different reading and interest levels to promote vocabulary development as well as independent reading. Classroom dictionaries and thesauri should not remain on shelves. Provide formal instruction on the benefits and uses of these great references.

Educators should involve parents in the vocabulary development of their children. Let parents know how important vocabulary development and growth is. Encourage them to read to their children, play word games with them, and explain the meaning of specific words when their children ask questions at home, in stores, or during other situations when they are together. Reading and discussing informational texts such as newspapers, nonfiction texts, magazines, and reference books can engage parents and older children in vocabulary development. Further, inform parents of the influence that vocabulary and concept development have on reading comprehension.

Vocabulary and word recognition also impact reading fluency. Teachers are cautioned not to confuse speed of reading with reading fluency. Reading fluency refers to processing surface-level text in order to achieve an understanding of the text. Accurate word decoding, processing to achieve meaning, and separating the text into syntactically and semantically correct parts are the dimensions of reading fluency. The area where a child is most deficient should determine the instruction used. Students need to be aware of what fluent reading sounds like. This requires providing repeated exposure, modeling, and read-aloud opportunities on the part of the teacher and practice on the part of the student.

We know that students need to widely expand their reading vocabularies because vocabulary strongly impacts communication, comprehension, and reading fluency and makes children successful readers. Classroom libraries, school libraries, public libraries, and bookstores are places where this can happen. Children, young and old, should have chances to select their own reading material based on their interests.

Schools are encouraged to bring book fairs to their institutions to provide exposure to appropriate literature and an opportunity for students to select their own reading material based on personal choice. Book fairs are also a way to reach readers who do not have opportunities to visit public libraries or bookstores.

Generally, when selecting a book fair for your school, choose one that offers hundreds of quality books at a variety of price ranges, interest levels, and reading levels. Schools will often earn funds and receive books and reading materials from the profits generated by a book fair. In addition, when parents accompany their children to a book fair, they connect with their child's reading interests while experiencing a rewarding reading event.

Numerous book fairs are available to choose from. Look for one that meets the needs of your students and your school. Begin your search with Scholastic Books and Schwabe Books. Both companies offer a variety of bookmobiles and allow schools to preview the books. In addition, Scholastic offers a guide to help families select books together and recognize the important reading stages.

As students progress through school, the texts and materials they are expected to read become more difficult and require additional new reading skills to meet with success. In general, secondary educators are not sufficiently trained to address the literacy needs of secondary students. There is also little room in a secondary curriculum to accommodate the needs of these struggling readers.

To combat the problem of adolescent illiteracy, it is suggested that schools build literacy classes into the existing curriculum where struggling readers can receive strategies to help them with their deficiencies. If this is not possible due to a lack of staffing or funding, offer professional development for all teachers to acquire some common reading strategies to assist students with the content presented in the various curriculums the school is using. By applying reading strategies school-wide, struggling students have a chance to achieve some understanding in each of their classes.

The research on adolescent literacy identifies some of the most effective strategies for educators to choose from when dealing with students who are not proficient readers.

Make sure to make the students a part of their own growth process. Share reading test scores and results from various reading assessments, and give students the responsibility of tracking their progress. Teach them how to interpret the data so they are able to determine their individual strengths and weaknesses. Allow them some say in what areas of improvement they want to focus on. When we give our students choices, they are more likely to work toward raising their test scores and ultimately value the important skill of reading.

In order to grow as a reader, students need to read often. The concept of sustained silent reading (SSR) is not new, but it is still very effective. It is not costly to implement, the time limit can be controlled, and it can be accomplished across the curriculum in all subject areas. SSR sends a message to students that reading is important, especially if the entire school makes a commitment to participate and teachers model good reading behavior during this time.

This kind of reading assists in vocabulary building, improves reading comprehension, and improves students' attitude toward reading for pleasure. Students should be required to carry a silent reading book with them at all times and read whenever possible during the school day, not just during the time allotted for SSR.

Working with individual words to build the skills necessary to read more complex texts is not as effective for older struggling readers as it is for younger struggling readers. Instead, offer these students plenty of opportunities to read printed material that already makes sense to them in all subject areas. If they are unable to read the main text for the course, provide them with a variety of resources or supplemental reading material that supports the main text. In this way, struggling students have a chance to come away with some understanding of the concepts covered in a particular class.

Work with struggling adolescent readers in small groups. This task is easier said than done at the middle and secondary levels, but is time well spent when it is possible. During small group interventions, allow students to verbalize the skills they have used to assist them in meeting success with reading material. This type of discussion is beneficial for all students in the group because it allows them to learn strategies from each other.

Good readers utilize strategies when they read; struggling readers need repeated practice when introduced to a new skill they lack. Adolescent readers require more new skills as they are asked to read many new forms of printed material, such as informational texts, different forms of technology, and different types of media.

Adolescent readers will need to learn a variety of reading strategies in order to fully comprehend more complex texts and new forms of printed information. Teachers should provide students with information on the new strategy at hand, when it should be used, how it is used, and why it is beneficial to use.

Developing and improving comprehension is critical for adolescents to make sense of the content presented in each of their classes. Activating and applying prior knowledge to text, generating thoughtful questions, thinking aloud, making inferences, constructing visuals, and summarizing are indicators that students comprehend. Tapping into prior knowledge is especially important when reading something new. Without background knowledge and interest in a piece, adolescents are reluctant to read it.

In addition, with such diverse populations of students in today's classrooms, teachers must also give students the opportunities to share their cultural beliefs and experiences when reading material that pertains to their ethnicity. A wide variety of multicultural literature should exist in classrooms for these students to utilize.

Effective comprehension instruction provides students with repeated practice using new strategies with a wide range of texts. Teachers should always model new strategies, and students should know why the strategies are beneficial to use. Students who read a variety of texts exhibit higher reading achievement.

Informational texts are read for authentic purposes because a student is prompted to extract specific bits of information to fulfill some kind of requirement, be it school-related or personal. Purposeful reading clues students into why the text is relevant and what the importance of the text is. When students are aware of what they are looking for, they are more likely to put increased effort into thinking about the text. When teachers take the guesswork out of a reading assignment, they are assisting students in strengthening their comprehension skills by giving them a focus.

Expository texts become more prevalent in middle and high school. Such texts include textbooks, reports, essays, and newspaper articles. For students to fully obtain maximum understanding, they must recognize the text's purpose and learn how to read through it to extract useful necessary pieces of information. Expository texts have unique structures, and students need to derive meaningful parts on their own through such techniques as:

- Identifying important, startling, or perplexing parts
- Highlighting key words and main ideas
- Summarizing in the margins of the pages

Expository texts build specific skills like sequencing, categorizing, comparing, contrasting, problem-solving, describing, and determining cause-and-effect relationships. Narrative texts, on the other hand, develop concepts like theme, plot, conflict, characterization, and setting. Fictional and nonfictional genres offer narrative texts that support the cultivation of these skills. Through skills such as questioning and correcting, visualizing, rereading, discussing, and forming literary, personal, and global connections, students can ascertain an author's purpose of a narrative text.

The launch of technology and living in the Information Age now require that students acquire a host of new skills and strategies to successfully read and gain insight from text on the Internet. Having a knowledge of general navigation techniques, search engines, and websites to access online reading, assessing the validity of online information, utilizing links, and synthesizing the vast amounts of information on websites are necessary to obtain the most from Information Age texts on the Internet. Multimedia presentations that combine audio, visual, animations, and text pose even more of challenge for students, thus requiring more teacher attention and intervention.

The Information Age also provides students with yet another type of literacy to engage in. Media literacy requires students to analyze real-world texts and news media from sources like television, movies, newspapers, magazines, and the Internet.

Media literacy involves four components: digital, art, oral, and written. Further, media literacy encompasses critical thinking and comprehension. Like other forms of literacy, students need to recognize its relevance to the everyday world, the author's purpose, and the intent of the piece. Typically, students are highly motivated by different forms of media with its verbal, visual, and auditory forms of expression.

Our role as educators is to teach students to master as much of the reading process as possible by exposing them to a wide variety of texts and using a wide range of strategies to meet the individual needs of our diverse student population. A truly literate student will result from a blending of former, current, and emerging literacy skills.

PRACTICES FOR PARENTS

As a child grows up, reading should become enjoyable as well as useful. Many factors influence a child's interest and performance in reading: a child's age, sex, grade level, and reading level. Exposure to books, availability and variety of reading material, reading material that a child can identify with, and a feeling of satisfaction while reading can also affect achievement.

There are many ways for parents to encourage good reading habits that ultimately lead to success.

Begin by creating a reading area in the home that is free of distraction and excess stimulation. Have a variety of reading materials available and easy to access in the home. Visit the local library or bookstores on a regular basis to uncover new and interesting reading material. Allow your child to make his or her own selections when appropriate. When material is too difficult for your child to read alone, read it together and discuss it.

Let your child know that reading is important. Model good reading behavior because children typically learn through example. Discover or create reading opportunities throughout the day that allow you and your child to read together. Some simple suggestions include reading road signs, store signs, grocery items, or anything that contains words. By doing this, you are showing your child how reading strongly affects his or her daily life.

Be mindful of your child's interests. Understanding what he or she likes and dislikes will make it easier for you to help your child to select books he or she is likely to enjoy. Knowing your child's interests will also assist you in choosing appropriate reading material for special occasions like birthdays, Christmas, and circumstances that deserve rewarding.

Encourage activities that are connected to reading. Diaries and journals filled with daily experiences in the form of words or pictures are a good start. Storytelling, guessing games, and writing stories, notes, or poems are a few more suggestions. Children frequently find it rewarding to view their own work in print.

How to Choose Books for Your Child

Throughout your child's lifetime, there will be numerous occasions when you will need to select books. Some of these occasions may involve choosing books for your own child; others may require you to make selections for young relatives or children of friends. Whatever the situation may be, parents can draw from a host of strategies when deciding on the most appropriate book for a child.

First of all, familiarize yourself with the interests and reading level of the child for whom you are choosing the book. Choose books that match his or her reading level as well as his or her current interests and hobbies. If possible, take the child with you when you go to select the book. Ask him or her what he or she would like to read about. Ask if the child has a favorite author, series, or genre. Then find a book that matches his or her responses. Libraries and bookstores employ people who are happy to assist parents and children in this way.

If you are unfamiliar with children's literature, ask your child's teacher, a local librarian, or bookstore clerk for book recommendations. Schools, libraries, and bookstores will often provide parents with booklists consisting of the most appropriate and popular books according to a child's grade level. Many of these lists can also be found by using the Internet. If you are still in doubt, draw from the classics and award-winning books as a starting place.

Selecting the best book for a child takes time. Be prepared to take the time to become familiar with the books you are choosing. Scan through the books and read some passages from the beginning, the middle, and the end. By doing this, parents can acquire a sense of what the book is about, its difficulty level, and its targeted audience.

Visiting the local library on a regular basis provides children and their parents with the newest literature published for children and adolescents. Parents themselves may even discover something new and interesting to read.

It is never too early to expose children to books. Babies and toddlers have the ability to listen and can respond to books with simple texts, good rhythms, rhymes, and word repetition. Babies and toddlers are often attracted to and stimulated by brightly colored pictures and objects found in books. Wordless books encourage young children to create their own stories to accompany them.

Purchase heavy-duty board books and cloth books for babies, toddlers, and young children. These kinds of books are more durable and will last over time. Many of these books are toylike and entertain young children with kinesthetic and pop-up-like features.

Children typically learn to read from the age of five to eight years old. Many children will learn to read even later. Older children who cannot read independently can understand and learn from picture books with a comprehensive story line and character development.

For children who are reading independently, books that have a straightforward story line with familiar words to them that are repeated throughout the book work best. These books are often labeled "Easy Readers" or "I Can Read Books" and state the book's reading level.

When a child enters third grade, choose books that are more complex for him or her. Be sure the book still contains familiar words, yet introduces some that are more challenging. By the time a child is nine years old, personality, personal preference, and special interests play a role in what that child will want to read. Parents need to keep this in mind when choosing informational books and novels at this level.

Parents should not be afraid to select a book that is recommended for an older reader if the subject matter meets with a child's interest level. Such a book can be read to a child while initiating the means for meaningful discussion around the content of the book. On the other hand, parents should not be reluctant to select a picture book that may seem more appropriate for a younger child. Many picture books are well illustrated with stimulating pictures and an interesting story and can initiate meaningful discussion as well.

Choosing books that relate to a family experience can also add to the benefits of reading while building strong family relationships. Planning for a vacation, expecting a new baby, moving to a new town or city, and coping with divorce, illness, or death are just some of the situations that may warrant books that can help children prepare for these experiences.

Books that have been deemed a classic should be part of everyone's reading experience. Many of the books that are part of this genre have been adapted for younger children or below-level readers. The Illustrated Classic Series is one popular series recommended for youngsters who are not yet able to read a classic in its original form.

Brand new books can be very costly to purchase, especially in hardcover form. If money is a concern, purchase desired books in paperback form. Reprints of hardcover titles are eventually widely available in paperback form. Internet sites such as Amazon.com offer a wide variety of new and used hardcover and paperback books that may be more economical.

Schools and libraries frequently offer book swaps for children to participate in. This is a great way to recycle books. Children are encouraged to clean out their bookshelves at home and bring the books they no longer want to the book swap to trade for other used books they have an interest in.

Schools and libraries also offer used book sales. Attending a used book sale can be a rewarding family activity because these sales offer books for young and old. This is another opportunity for parents to act as reading role models for their children in an inexpensive way.

Families are urged to take advantage of school book clubs like Scholastic Arrow or TAB whenever possible. These book clubs provide educators, parents, and students with information about the latest books and authors on a variety of levels on a monthly basis. The books available for purchase are often discounted and free of sales tax.

Utilizing book fairs, book swaps, garage or yard sales, and public library events are good ways to add books to a home library at an economical cost. The Internet is another notable source for accessing information about authors and books and provides secure sites for purchasing the books themselves.

When utilizing the Internet, choose sites for books that are updated on a regular basis. Search for book lists that have been compiled by book experts, librarians, and teachers, along with student input.

The cognitive function of reading was formulated approximately 5,500 years ago. Understanding how human beings learned to read allows today's educators and parents to perceive how children use their brains to make connections among the structures of vision, hearing, cognition, and language. It takes years for a young brain to develop the processes that attain and support comprehension, inferential and deductive reasoning, critical analysis, reflection, and insight.

Successful readers learn to extract meaning from text by applying prior knowledge as they question, analyze, and investigate. In turn, they build knowledge by moving beyond the words of the author to generate their own thoughts.

Today's students must develop the ability to apply their reading knowledge to a variety of texts in print and online. When educators help students to use their ability, they promote literacy and, at the same time, meet the needs of different individuals in a culture. When parents recognize the important contributions of both online and printed texts, they can support the schools in making students literate in these areas and prepare them for life in the twenty-first century.

Chapter 6

Building Self-Esteem

Our self-esteem or self-image is created by the set of beliefs or feelings that we have about ourselves. Patterns of self-esteem begin early in life. That is why parents play such an important role in promoting healthy self-esteem in their children.

Healthy self-esteem provides a child with the necessary mechanisms to face the challenges in life. Children who have high self-esteem seem to be able to handle conflict and resist negative pressures more easily. Children who have low self-esteem have more difficulty finding solutions to problems. Challenges create high levels of anxiety and frustration for them.

Self-esteem changes as a child grows. It is altered by new experiences and interactions with others. A child needs to experience a sense of achievement and, at the same time, experience a sense of love and recognition by those around him or her. That is why it is so important for parents to understand how much influence they have on fostering a sense of high or low self-esteem in their child.

Children spend significant amounts of time in a school setting. It is equally important for educators to understand the many roles they play during the school day and the effects these roles have on their students' self-esteem. Positions of school authority, guidance counselors, teachers, coaches, school nurses, psychologists, and academic specialists interact with students on different levels and in different ways, and they all have a profound impact on the way students feel about themselves.

This chapter is designed to show educators and parents how they can make a difference in shaping a child's self-esteem in a positive way.

ESSENTIALS FOR EDUCATORS

One of the most important academic areas greatly affected by a student's self-esteem is graduation. Approximately 68 percent of students who are currently enrolled in high school graduate, and 40 percent of those students move on to college. Although the average IQ for today's young adults continues to climb and their level of sophistication continues to grow, large numbers of students are not meeting with success before they even leave the school setting.

Research suggests that factors such as irrelevant curriculums, inadequate instructional approaches, hard-reaching government mandates, and living conditions outside of school attribute to school failure and dramatically impact a student's self-esteem.

Presently, the need for forming a connection between educators and students seems to have become more important than the need for students to form a connection with curriculum. Forming positive relationships between educators and students will help students to recognize their potential to achieve. Today's educators must convey a message to students that they not only care about their academic learning, but they also care about them as individuals.

When students feel valued as people, they are less likely to use substances; engage in fighting, bullying, and vandalism; suffer from suicidal thoughts; become pregnant; have a high rate of absenteeism; or drop out of school. Instead, they are more likely to acquire a heightened sense of self-esteem, do well academically, and graduate.

What can educators do to enhance the self-esteem in our young people so they not only feel good about themselves but also succeed academically? Several common factors are present in the research regarding self-esteem and academic success.

First and foremost, students need to feel connected to the academic environment they are immersed in. Students acquire a sense of belonging when they feel their school is a safe haven, consider the school rules to be reasonable and fair, believe their teachers care about them, consider learning opportunities to be meaningful, establish friendships with peers, and take part in activities and clubs offered by the school.

Teachers can create such a culture by making the course content applicable to students' ability levels and interest levels. Whenever possible, involve students in the decision-making process when choosing course content and requirements beyond what the curriculum dictates. Students will value the learning experience more when they have a say in the design.

Students come to school with not only academic needs but also emotional needs. Teachers are challenged to find ways to address both of these realms. Traditionally, teachers have been trained to develop an expertise in academics and find it difficult to attend to the affective domain. A lack of understanding of students' social and emotional needs and a full focus on academic needs will result in failure for many students. We will never reach our students academically until we understand their backgrounds and life experiences. Like it or not, the schools have become the support systems for many of our students.

Teachers and school personnel can gain insights that will guide them in developing lessons and activities that will ultimately support student learning. To begin, ask students to share what they think about themselves, their school, and their peers. Their responses will often be very candid and reveal what their social and emotional needs are. Furthermore, their responses will identify students who feel overwhelmed and experience low self-esteem. Educators can then plan ways to address these needs individually or in a group setting.

Students desire teachers who will listen to their needs. When a teacher acknowledges the demands of real life, students view this teacher as an adult who not only cares about their academic success, but also cares about them as individuals. This kind of a teacher can have a great influence on students and motivate them toward academic success. One way to achieve this is to teach students how to handle the pressures of everyday life with examples of how to balance school, family, and social responsibilities. Then, whenever possible, provide different means for these at-risk students to achieve academic outcomes.

Project-based learning and hands-on, life-related learning activities have been shown to motivate at-risk students. Equally effective have been service-learning projects where students engage in projects that benefit the community. The end results give students a personal sense of satisfaction. In addition, educators, parents, peers, and members of the community often recognize students for the effort they have demonstrated.

Most students enjoy working with their peers. Teachers should incorporate cooperative learning opportunities for content that lends itself to this type of learning strategy. Feeling a part of a small group also fosters self-esteem. Varied instructional methods such as hands-on tasks and assignments are also important to consider for students who learn best by such an approach. They deserve to be successful and feel good about themselves.

Whatever the approach, teachers need to convey high academic standards and clear expectations to students and parents. Learning material must be aligned with these standards and expectations.

Parental partnerships are vital for student success. Further, these partnerships help to create a culture for success. Offer parent sessions to introduce them to the curriculum, school and classroom rules, and school and classroom expectations. This type of school-to-home knowledge heightens parental awareness and encourages them to be more involved in their children's education beyond homework completion. Ask parents to talk with their children at home about how new skills and concepts outlined in the curriculum pertain to school and how they can be applied at home.

Additional sessions on important adolescent topics are also suggested for parents to attend. Sessions pertaining to drug and alcohol abuse, peer pressure, divorce, grief, and loss are a starting point. Invite members of the faculty and staff to attend these informational sessions as well to deepen relationships and intensify partnerships.

When students transition from elementary school to middle school and from middle school to high school, create opportunities for sending and receiving teachers to meet to discuss issues that may arise during the transition period. Bringing faculty together to share curriculums and grade-level expectations and requirements will ensure a smoother transition for students.

Periods of transition can be most unsettling for students. Activities that help to reduce anxiety for students are extremely worthwhile. They will not only help at the point of transition, but also extend beyond that time and give students a better chance of settling in and meeting with success as the school year progresses.

Useful activities include orientations, student shadowing, school visitations, and summer sessions that address issues such as study skills, time management, and general information about the new school experience. Providing students with occasions for incoming students to develop positive relationships with older students and other incoming students will also reduce anxiety for the newcomers and promote a positive self-image for those students who are assisting.

Adolescents enjoy social interaction. During transitional periods, friendships are often disrupted. These disruptions can interfere substantially with school success. Offering opportunities for social interaction affords students the chance for making new friends as well as sustaining old friendships. Many schools offer relationship-building programs during the summer so that new students can enjoy the full benefits of the school experience from the start.

Support for students cannot end after a transition period. Mentoring and advisory programs should provide all students with ongoing support throughout the school year. Such programs are mandated in many states because of their positive results. Teachers, counselors, administrators, members of the faculty and staff, parents, and members of the community can act as mentors or advisors to students.

Recruiting adults from outside of the school is critical for some institutions where the ratio of adults to students is especially low. School guidance counselors, psychologists, and social workers are in high demand. Much of a guidance counselor's time is now spent scheduling courses, assisting students with college preparation, coordinating test-taking procedures and results, and fulfilling contractual duties. With so many students in crisis, psychologists and social workers also lack the time to sufficiently address the problems and needs of today's youth.

Partnering students with a caring adult will increase a feeling of academic and social security, especially for students with low self-esteem. Strong relationships with adults have been known to raise self-esteem and academic success for all students. Once partnerships are established, meeting times need to be offered on a regular basis. Activities need to be designed to increase self-awareness, decision-making skills, and responsible academic and social behavior so students develop the ability to make appropriate academic decisions as well as healthy life decisions.

Feeling a connection to a caring adult is essential for its positive effects on students. Feeling a connection to the school is equally important. We want our students to succeed and graduate from high school with the skills they need to go on to college or support themselves if they choose not to do so. Students who drop out of school have a negative impact on the economy and the town or city in which they live. Students who drop out of school are more likely to encounter unemployment, face imprisonment, or need government assistance. Low self-esteem usually accompanies these factors.

Educators must search for ways for students to become excited about learning and recognize the value of an education. Low-income students, high-mobility students, low achievers, students with a high rate of absenteeism, and students who have experienced a fair amount of grade retention are especially at high risk for possessing a low self-esteem and dropping out of school. These populations should be targeted and provided with information on how dropping out of school will impact their future.

Research tells us that students are dropping out of school at younger ages. Many of these dropouts remain unemployed without the skills or knowledge to gain employment. Of those students who are engaged in the workforce, a significant amount of these individuals earn wages close to the poverty line for a family. Still others do not even come close to this level.

A number of approaches are available for educators to draw from to reduce the dropout rate. When interventions are put into practice early on, it increases the chances for future success. It will be difficult to implement all of the suggestions due to time constraints; contractual obligations; or lack of money, resources, and staffing. Perhaps some will be appropriate or at least able to be modified to fit the needs of individual school districts.

Many districts have the resources to offer after-school tutoring programs for struggling students. It is important to develop criteria for eligibility as well as a way to measure the program's effectiveness. For students who do not fit into the traditional school mold, schools have been known to partner with local technical schools, colleges, and universities. Students who require a greater challenge may even be able to take advantage of programs offered by institutions of higher education. Such practices support the need for aligning coursework with students' unique learning styles.

It is important for educators to recognize that many of their students live in difficult situations. They encounter numerous economic, social, and life-threatening issues on a daily basis. Such issues can dominate their lives and make it difficult for them to engage in academic affairs. The teacher and the classroom structure are key factors in keeping these students interested in participating in school and completing an education.

The teacher must acknowledge students as people with real-life problems and fears. Whenever possible, academics need to be structured so they involve students personally and intellectually. If personal issues are acknowledged in some way, students will have room to focus on learning. We must help students move beyond a feeling of low self-esteem about their ability or accepting failure as a strategy for getting through their educational career.

Matching students' voices and individual learning styles with a host of learning activities and formats may be the answer to engaging struggling students who appear uninterested in school. Use what students tell us about themselves as a catalyst for their studies. Learning opportunities and material that is authentic and engaging will motivate students.

Educators should be mindful of the ways in which they approach students to gather information about them or react to a situation they are involved in. Address students respectfully and as individuals. Do not assume, for example, that all struggling students from low-income families have the same needs and concerns. Never single out students in front of others. This can be difficult to do if a student acts out continuously. Singling out a student only feeds into the problem and sends a message to the student that he or she is a failure.

Whenever possible, give a student some control over deciding projects, classwork, and grades. When you discover a student's strength, focus on it, and use it to guide you when preparing projects or lessons. Provide examples of finished products, and model strategies that students can utilize to gain ideas and confidence from. Students enjoy classes that incorporate their nonacademic interests as well as opportunities that link them to the community.

Hands-on learning opportunities linked with students' interests have always had positive results and hold strong with today's students. It is yet another strategy to draw from for struggling students. If you are unable to help a student, suggest someone who can, and assist the student in making the arrangements to connect with him or her. The right support coupled with the right instruction raises self-esteem and results in increased school attendance and achievement.

Integrating the arts into the curriculum has also been known to yield positive outcomes. Recent evidence reveals that the arts can be an especially powerful tool to engage struggling students. Subjects that fall within the realm of the arts tend to offer students more authentic learning experiences. Arts-related courses allow students to identify with their interests and express themselves as individuals.

Many districts have begun to incorporate the arts such as art, music, and drama into other subjects with enormous success. To assist with this endeavor, districts have utilized community resources. Forming partnerships with local colleges or universities that offer art education and employ the services of local artists are a start. In addition, parents tend to express an interest in their children when they are involved in celebrating their successes through the arts. Parents seem to be more willing to attend performances and exhibitions when their children are involved in them.

Reaching struggling students is a challenge for today's educators. Most of these students possess low self-esteem and have lived with hardship and failure for much of their academic careers. Educators must realize that they cannot change the world, but they can make a difference with the students they see on a daily basis. Focusing on student interests, offering real-world experiences, seeking out available funds, and taking advantage of community resources just might improve a student's self-esteem and put that student on the path toward academic success.

PRACTICES FOR PARENTS

Self-esteem is an emotion that has been studied extensively. Most will agree that parents and other adults who are involved with children largely contribute to their development physically and emotionally. Within the emotional realm lies self-esteem. The foundation for a healthy or unhealthy sense of self-esteem begins during infancy when babies establish attachments to the adults who care for them.

Children who acquire a positive sense of self-esteem feel good about themselves. They feel cherished by the adults in their lives as well as by their peer groups. They enjoy feeling a part of a peer group and comfortable participating in it. As children become older, they become sensitive to the reactions of their peer groups. These reactions will influence the way children feel about themselves.

Children who acquire a negative sense of self-esteem do not feel good about themselves. They often experience feelings of self-doubt. Situations that allow for prejudice and discrimination contribute to a negative sense of self-esteem.

Different cultures, ethnic groups, families, and members of the community may share different viewpoints about what constitutes self-esteem. For example, some may consider physical appearance or certain attributes displayed by boys and girls as factors that contribute to self-esteem.

Children do not always feel good about themselves in every situation. In situations where children experience defeat resulting in low self-esteem, it is important for parents to help with discovering the coping skills necessary for dealing with feelings of defeat. Avoid criticism and making statements that are judgmental and shameful. Children need to know that they are still loved and accepted, even when they are not successful. Praise children when they meet with success, but also offer praise for the effort put into a challenge, even if they do not attain the desired result.

Without question, parents play a strong role in the development of self-esteem in their children. In fact, parents are typically the first adults that children learn to trust and rely on to satisfy their needs. As time goes on, children gradually feel wanted, valued, and loved by their parents, feelings that are essential for developing healthy self-esteem.

What can parents do to foster a healthy self-esteem and sustain these feelings over time? Much of what has always been believed to contribute to positive and negative self-esteem continues to hold strong today. As an aid to parents, the most important methods for supporting and sustaining positive self-esteem are highlighted.

Begin by being a positive role model for your children. They will mirror what they see in you. Be honest about your own abilities and limitations without focusing on your shortcomings.

Help your children to set accurate and individualistic goals. Teach them to evaluate themselves in a realistic way. This will not guarantee that your child will always make the right choices, but it will help them to select ambitions that are more likely to result in outcomes that will encourage positive feelings. Recognize when children make the right choices. They will likely continue to do so in the future.

Support activities that encourage cooperation rather than competition. Whenever competitive situations do arise, teach your children to try their best and be satisfied with their best effort. Avoid negative feedback when they fail. Tell your children that you are proud of them, regardless of what the result may be. Show affection through gestures and notes.

Make your home a safe and nurturing place. A home environment where children do not feel safe should be examined closely for warning signs. Physical and verbal abuse, physical fighting, and verbal arguments will enhance low self-esteem. Be mindful of such indicators, and address them immediately.

Assigning responsibilities such as chores is a practical way to foster healthy self-esteem. Begin with two or three tasks, and add to them later. Permit children to choose chores they would like to complete rather than always deciding for them. This type of responsibility makes children accountable and often extends outside of the home in situations that call for dependable individuals.

Using a framework can assist parents in identifying problem areas and developing plans for improving them to promote healthy self-esteem. Harris Clemes and Reynold Bean developed a notable framework after completing their own research on building self-esteem.

The framework consists of four conditions of self-esteem that include connectiveness, uniqueness, power, and models. A discrepancy in one or more of the conditions may result in poor self-esteem. This framework encompasses the most significant and relevant research findings in the area of self-esteem. Parents are encouraged to make use of the suggestions presented.

Develop children's sense of connectiveness through physical touch and loving words. Provide and participate in situations where children feel like important and valued members of the family, neighborhood, community, sports team, church, or school. Teach your child effective social and conversational skills to ensure positive connections with others. Do this through modeling, direct teaching, and guided practice. Share family stories with children. Tell them about their ancestors, their heritage, and their nationality to establish a connection with their roots.

Develop children's sense of uniqueness by providing opportunities to discover their own special talents. Allow children to express themselves in their own way. Be respectful of their thoughts and feelings so they will learn to have the same respect for others. Recognize and appreciate children's curiosity, creativity, and imagination by suggesting learning opportunities that will allow for further exploration of these qualities. Show the joy that can come from learning by sharing your own interests and experiences as a parent and unique individual.

Develop children's sense of power by offering the support, teaching, and resources necessary for them to be successful with accomplishing realistic goals. Give your child responsibilities in the family. Ask for their input in decisions that affect them. When learning a new skill, provide children with numerous opportunities to practice and master that skill. Teach them the skills necessary to cope with failure. Help children to be effective problem-solvers and decision-makers by providing them with the skills needed to prioritize and think about a course of action. Insist that they consider the consequences before taking action.

Develop children's sense of modeling by demonstrating appropriate behaviors through your own actions. Distinguish between right and wrong by discussing your own values and beliefs when you encounter a dilemma and make a decision. Persuade children to apply strong values in their own decision-making ability. Offering a broad range of experiences will build confidence when children come upon new experiences. Help children set major and minor goals for themselves. Specify your expectations as well as the standards and consequences for their behavior.

Taking an active role in nourishing and supporting high self-esteem will result in children who act independently, assume responsibility, take pride in their accomplishments, tolerate frustration, handle peer pressure appropriately, attempt new challenges, and handle their emotions appropriately. These behaviors will not only be seen at home, but will also transcend to the community and the school.

School and school-related activities greatly impact children's self-esteem. Ten to twenty percent of students are retained at least once in their school era. That is why it is necessary for parents to be involved in their children's education. Helping children to shift negative beliefs about themselves into thinking positively about themselves is vital at any age. Take the time to discuss your child's progress, answer questions about his or her concerns, and think of alternatives that lead to success.

Take an interest in your child's education. Parental involvement leads to better grades, improved test scores, increased attendance, more positive attitudes and behavior, and higher graduation rates. Talk with children about schoolwork, teachers, friends, and the sports or activities they are involved in. Be confident that your involvement makes a difference in the way your child feels about himself or herself and his or her academic success.

Know your child's interests at school. Take full advantage of the information provided by the school and your child's teacher through newsletters and online. Participate in activities that are offered, and attend sporting events that your child is involved in.

Take part in seminars or workshops that deal with topics such as drugs, alcohol, divorce, grief, and loss. Forming parent-school relationships help children to feel better about school and are more likely to get involved themselves.

Surf the Internet for advice and guides that offer practical advice to parents about children's emotional development and the latest research on self-esteem to better support children at home and at school. Such information will assist parents in coping with the many changes that children experience while growing up.

Here are some simple self-esteem builders that parents and children can draw from to build confidence, thoughtfulness, and positive relationships:

- Work on creating a scrapbook together. Include items that give your child identity, show what your child is capable of, and show their accomplishments and experiences over time.
- Read the same book or watch the same television program together. Take turns sharing thoughts and feelings about it.
- Include children in grown-up discussions they are able to contribute to.
- Discuss ways children can do special things for others. Plan and arrange for them to carry out these ideas.
- Plan and take a special road trip together.
- Send your child a note or an e-mail just to say that you care.
- Have a family dinner. Plan and prepare it together.

Parents are commonly the first and most important influence on a child's self-esteem. Parents must not only show love and affection, but also allow children to feel capable by not always solving problems for them, coddling them, making decisions for them, or speaking for them.

Instead, assign responsibilities they are capable of fulfilling. Show appreciation for interests and effort. Talk with children about their thoughts, feelings, and ideas. Be a good listener. Stay involved in the education process so that children are academically successful. Finally, it is important for children to know you care. Reassure them that you still support and accept them even when failure occurs. Children with high self-esteem are confident and much more capable of dealing with the many challenges life has to offer.

SUGGESTIONS FOR STUDENTS

Many students wish they could change the way they feel about themselves, but are unaware of how to do so. Many students experience negative feelings about themselves, like doubt, inadequacy, and shame. As time goes on, these kinds of feelings intensify and consume students. They begin to apply them to everything they do. Such emotions constitute a low, unhealthy self-esteem that prevents individuals from moving forward to meet with success. This section addresses ways for students to gain more control over their emotions to attain a positive, healthy self-esteem.

As a student, you experience many factors in your daily life that affect your self-concept. These factors are present both in and out of school. Your self-concept is the view you have of yourself. It includes your perception of your abilities, skills, and talents.

Your self-concept begins to form at a very young age. Your parents or guardians have the greatest influence at this stage in your life. Their words and actions toward you have lasting effects. As you grow older, your skills, talents, and abilities mold your self-concept as you recognize your strengths and weaknesses. Focus on your strengths and what you enjoy doing. Seeing yourself in a positive light will help you to feel good about yourself and contribute to a positive self-concept.

Positive messages from others also help to improve an individual's self-image. Messages from parents, family members, peers, and educators reinforce your beliefs about yourself. Sending positive messages can work in two ways. When you are supportive of others, they are likely to be supportive of you. You can achieve this by offering words of encouragement when others need it or congratulating them for a job well done. Positive messages help to develop and reinforce a positive self-concept.

If you have a positive self-concept, you are also likely to have a high level of self-esteem. Although these two concepts are closely linked, self-esteem is more of a measure of the degree to which you like and respect yourself. High self-esteem means you have confidence in yourself and are ready to meet challenges that emerge. When things go wrong, you have the ability to be resilient and work through obstacles that surface. You also have the ability to cope with failure and disappointment more positively. You believe in the words, "If at first you don't succeed, try again."

A positive self-concept, along with high self-esteem, are important components of your emotional health. Try the following suggestions to build and enhance these components:

- Acquire a realistic view of yourself. List your strengths and weaknesses. Focus on what you do well.
- Have confidence in yourself. Believe in yourself and your abilities. Try new things. Develop your talents and abilities.
- Accept compliments and encouragement from others, helping you to recognize your strengths. Praise yourself whenever you deserve it.

- Set realistic goals and expectations for yourself. Work toward achieving them to gain a sense of accomplishment. Self-evaluate yourself, and refocus if you need to.
- Remember that nobody is perfect.
- Seek out friends who will accept you and offer support and encouragement during hard times.
- Ignore harmful remarks or strange looks from others, and move on because they are often not worth focusing on.

Is it easy to change your self-concept and build self-esteem? No, but it is worth the effort to try. The results will be beneficial to you. Examine yourself, and change the things you do not like about yourself. If you work at this, but fail to make progress, seek out the help of a qualified individual like a teacher, advisor, counselor, school psychologist, or social worker.

Take pride in your individuality. Appreciate your uniqueness, and use your distinctive characteristics to respond to others in favorable and productive ways. Be happy for others when they succeed.

Think positively about yourself. Accept your strengths and weaknesses. Everyone has them. Adopt a can-do attitude, and encourage yourself to achieve your personal goals. Try to learn new skills to meet your goals. Take pride in your accomplishments.

Finally, take time out for self-reflection. Think about your thoughts and feelings. Involve yourself in activities that you enjoy doing on your own to get in touch with yourself. Do what makes you happy and fulfilled. Trust your inner thoughts and feelings, and act on what you think is correct.

Above all, be yourself. Do not try to be someone you are not. Be proud of who you are, and appreciate your own special talents and contributions. Learn to love the unique person you are. Accept failure, and learn from your mistakes. Accept the person you are. The people in your life who truly love and care about you will accept you, too.

A child's self-esteem begins to form early in life. Healthy self-esteem development is an important component of academic success, but it also contributes to so much more in an individual's life.

Parents and educators are key players in the development of self-esteem. Parents are the first builders of self-esteem. They are responsible for fulfilling their children's needs and establishing a home environment that nurtures, teaches good choices, and celebrates successes. Educators are responsible for establishing an academic environment where students feel safe, a sense of belonging, and connected to the learning.

Once children reach a certain age, they become capable of changing the way they feel about themselves. They are responsible for seeking ways to build upon their talents, form strong peer relationships, and take pride in being the special individuals they are.

Forming partnerships that work toward healthy self-esteem is the most effective means to positively influence our children and young people and mold them into individuals who will succeed in life.

Chapter 7

School Violence: Bullying

School violence, especially the area of bullying, has long been a serious and persistent problem in education. It is an area in which schools must focus attention and instruction. Bullying can have devastating effects on students' emotional security and their academics. All students, whether they are victims, witnesses, or bullies, are impacted. Yet, bullying is an issue that is minimized and rarely addressed by educators.

This chapter will serve as a resource to educate school personnel about the harmful effects of bullying. It will address the causes and signs of bullying and will provide a variety of approaches that can be used to assist victims, bystanders, and the bullies themselves. Because cyberbullying has entered the realm of school violence, this chapter will expand its resources to include this area.

Bullying extends into the home. The home environment may be a contributing factor, or it may be the recipient of bullying when a child falls victim to a bully and requires the support of the family. When the bully is an actual part of the family, it puts a tremendous strain on family dynamics. Like educators, parents need to be aware of the causes and signs of bullying. They also need to be equipped with strategies to guide their child in the right direction when the issue of bullying surfaces. Information to help parents and their children cope with this area of school violence can also be found within this chapter.

ESSENTIALS FOR EDUCATORS

Bullying can include physical, verbal, or sexual abuse and can extend to social ostracism. The victimized individual is typically weaker and more vulnerable than the tormenter.

Boys torment more than girls do, and the bullying is more physical. Girls gravitate more toward verbal tactics like spreading rumors or other acts that damage friendships. Teasing tends to be the most common form of bullying for both boys and girls in elementary and middle school. Studies reveal that children who bully are more inclined to engage in criminal behaviors as adults.

Bullying can consist of direct and indirect acts that are physical or verbal in nature. Hitting, kicking, pushing, and choking are ways a bully may attack a victim physically and are considered forms of direct bullying. Verbal attacks, also known as harassment, can involve name-calling, threatening, taunting, and malevolent teasing. Forms of indirect bullying include spreading rumors, making faces or gesturing, controlling friendships, and interfering with the movement of others by deliberately standing in their way. Indirect bullying is more subtle and harder to detect.

Direct and indirect forms of bullying can also be sexual or racial in nature. Inappropriate touching, staring at an individual's body, and sexual comments and gestures constitute sexual bullying. Racial slurs, inappropriate comments about the color of one's skin, and graffiti written to degrade one's ethnic background are considered racial bullying. Anytime bullying takes place, the victimized person is made to feel fearful, anxious, and uncomfortable.

The statistics involving bullying are eye-opening. One in seven students in the United States report being bullied daily, and approximately 170,000 skip school every day because of issues related to bullying. One in four students who bully will be involved in the criminal system by the time they are thirty years old and are six times more likely to have a criminal record by the age of twenty-four than the rest of the student population. Between 75 and 90 percent of students indicate they were severely bullied at some time in their educational career. Fifteen percent of students in grades four through eight reveal feelings of anxiety on a regular basis because of bullying.

Clearly, educators cannot ignore the data. Many districts have become proactive in establishing programs to address the issue of bullying. The goal of any anti-bullying program should be to educate faculty, staff members, and students about the causes and harmful effects of bullying as well as the strategies the entire school community can make use of to create and maintain a bully-free environment.

To begin to understand bullying, it is important to realize why people, regardless of age, torment others. People are not born bullies. Bullying is not a phase that young people go through while growing up. It is a way for individuals to have power over others, and the reasons and means for doing so varies from person to person.

Some individuals bully to gain popularity. Bullies are often insecure and intimidate others to disguise these feelings. When they bully, they feel powerful and in charge. Some seek attention or harbor feelings of jealousy toward those they victimize. They bully to attain recognition or the possessions of others. People may bully because they have fallen victim to a bully themselves. They begin to pick on others because it is the only way they know how to deal with their feelings.

The way young people are treated at home and at school contribute to the causes of bullying. Home factors that lead to bullying include the absence of parental involvement or interaction, lack of praise for accomplishments or encouragement for shortfalls, and a shortage of affection. Young people learn by example. Forceful, physical discipline in the home, exposure to large amounts of television violence, and easy access to guns all contribute to bullying. Male bullies tend to continue this type of behavior in adulthood. They are at a greater risk for criminal behavior, domestic abuse, child abuse, and sexual harassment.

Permissive homes where there is little supervision and too much freedom lack boundaries and give young people a sense of freedom to do as they please. This carries over to situations outside of the home. These youngsters enjoy having the upper hand and bully to maintain it.

Certain school factors create an environment that promotes bullying. Schools and classrooms that lack discipline, high expectations, and strategies to effectively deal with bullying have a higher incidence of it. Low visibility in hallways and remote areas in the school will also make it easier for the tormenting of students to occur. Schools that have negative expectations and poor relationships among students and educators are likely to have a greater number of bullying issues.

Schools and classrooms need to establish and maintain structured environments. This can be accomplished with a strong schoolwide discipline system consisting of rules and consequences that are enforced consistently. High levels of adult visibility are also necessary to prevent acts of bullying. Faculty and staff should be observable in locations where bullying is likely to occur. Hallways, bathrooms, cafeterias, locker rooms, and recreational fields are places where victims are targeted the most.

The victims of bullies tend to be smaller in stature. They are often unpopular among their peers. They are students who do not defend themselves or seek the help of adults. Certain characteristics of girls make them more vulnerable to a bully, including a distinctive facial appearance, an unattractive appearance, and an attractive appearance. Girls who are overweight, well developed, sensitive and cry easily, high-achieving, talented, or homosexual are more likely to fall victim to a bully.

On the other hand, certain characteristics make boys the target of a bully. Poor peer relationships, a short temper, clothing, or an inclination toward the arts tends to place boys at risk. Boys who are non-athletic, physically weak, or socially unaccepted by peers make them equally at risk.

Bullying can make young people feel lonely, unhappy, scared, and unsafe. Their self-confidence and self-esteem plummets, and they believe there is something wrong with them. They may become physically sick with headaches and stomachaches and do not want to attend school anymore. Statistics show that young people who have a history of abuse and are victimized by bullying have a greater tendency to use guns.

Bullies will torment their victims any place where they think they can get away with it. Bathrooms, locker rooms, hallways, stairwells, the cafeteria, and any other areas in a school that lack adult supervision are popular locations. Playgrounds and buses are also places that bullies target. Bullying is not always subtle. The presence of an audience reinforces the act of bulling. Peers who join in physically or verbally or simply watch without intervening support a bully and encourage this type of torture to continue.

Encourage students to report bullying incidents they witness. Like the victims, out of fear, bystanders are reluctant to tell those in authority what they have observed. Educators must create safe ways for bystanders and victims to disclose information, including actual names of bullies. Further, students need reassurance that their disclosures will be taken seriously and acted upon.

Conduct bullying awareness discussions to allow students the opportunity to discuss their feelings and to ask questions surrounding the issue of bullying. Hold schoolwide assemblies to disseminate information about the signs, causes, and consequences of bullying. Have individuals available in the school who can meet with students one-on-one to discuss their fears and offer strategies on how to deal with situations involving bullies. Above all, convey a strong message to the victims of bullying that it is not their fault and nobody deserves to be bullied.

When bullies confront victims, suggest that they do not panic. Instead, advise them to avoid engaging in violence, and walk away. Tell them to agree with what the bully has to say to avoid an altercation. Students should attempt to seek out an adult or teacher. Usually, a bully will not continue in the presence of an adult. Recommend that students ignore a bully or pretend to not notice the bullying. Without a challenge, bullies will often give up and stop.

Educate faculty and staff on the causes of bullying. Teach them to recognize the signs. Be on the lookout for students who brag about being tough and boss other students around. Be aware of students who pick on other students, belittle them, harass them, or call them names. Once bullies are identified, have strategies in place for educators to draw from to intervene and correct the situation. Teach methods to victims and bystanders about how to handle themselves and prevent bullying from continuing. Be sure students are aware of the difference between tattling and reporting an incident that will ultimately help another.

Students who witness acts of bullying often feel helpless and find it difficult to deal with. They want to help the victim in some way, but are unsure of how to do so. Students should be aware that they can help in many ways.

First of all, bystanders should know that it is not appropriate to watch the act of violence or to join in. This strengthens the power of the bully and provides a much-desired audience. Instead, bystanders should support the targeted individual by asking the bully to stop the intimidation. Bystanders can show other acts of kindness toward the victim by suggesting they leave together and then allow the victim to talk about the incident. Finally, bystanders should report incidents of bullying to a teacher, faculty member, or principal while the event is occurring or afterward.

Students who bully are often disliked in school and not accepted by their peer group. They are tolerated by their peers out of fear. Many of these students grow up to be adults with criminal records, and many of them have altercations with the law as young adults.

Bullies need role models who can influence them positively. For many, school is the only place where these role models exist. It is up to educators to create and maintain a positive school environment. This includes developing relationships with all students, including bullies. This can be difficult for educators to establish with undesirable students. To make this easier, educators can start with simple things like greeting these students when they arrive in the morning or when they arrive in class. Compliment them whenever possible. Talk to them about their personal interests. Above all, educators should understand the dynamics of bullying in order to deal with them successfully.

When educators deal with bullies in a positive light, their self-concept and self-esteem improves, and they become less concerned with intimidating others in order to feel special. Recognize talents and accomplishments. Provide public and private venues to show off student achievements. Create situations for these students to be successful.

School bullying is everyone's responsibility. Schools must become proactive and establish an anti-bullying policy that includes zero tolerance. Educators, parents, and students should take an active role in creating it. Students and faculty should be surveyed, and the anti-bullying policy should be reviewed regularly to determine if the school's interventions are effective. Design surveys that collect information about frequency of incidents, students who bully, and where and when they bully. Feedback is an important tool to use to assess how successful the school is at preventing bullying.

With a strong commitment to eliminate the problem of bullying, the number of cases will be drastically reduced, and the overall school climate will become more positive. The school will become a safe haven for students to learn and grow.

PRACTICES FOR PARENTS

Bullying is a serious problem. It exists in all schools, regardless of the location. The effects are harmful physically, emotionally, and academically. It is not a topic that parents routinely discuss with their children because most children will not report being bullied. They are fearful of the repercussions.

How can you tell if your child is a victim of bullying? When children are bullied at school, they devise ways to avoid going there. They display signs of anxiety, have trouble sleeping, and experience nightmares. Victims may also develop physical symptoms and complain about headaches or stomachaches, especially when they have to attend school. If you notice that some of your child's possessions are missing or damaged, these could be signs that a bully is bothering your child.

A parent's first reaction is to confront his or her child by directly asking about certain behaviors. A direct confrontation may not be the best way to make children open up. An indirect approach may be much more successful. Begin with general questions about school. Ask your child how he or she spends his or her nonstructured time in places like the cafeteria, locker room, hallways, playground, and bus.

Share your own experiences with teasing or bullying when you were a child. Tell your child how you felt at the time and how you handled the situations. Try role-playing with your child. Re-create situations involving various aspects of bullying. Brainstorm nonaggressive ways to respond to the situations together. Approaches that involve reporting aggression and abuse, remaining with a group of friends, and keeping within sight of adults and teachers are recommended.

If you are concerned about the responses and suspect that bullying is taking place, make some inquiries at school. Seek out teachers and other educators who deal with your child to determine if they have witnessed any episodes of bullying. At the same time, ask about the school's anti-bullying policy and the consequence for the mistreatment of others.

If your child is the victim of a bully, you can take some measures to help your child deal with the trauma of what is happening. First, remain calm, and be an active listener. Allow your child the time needed. Discuss nonviolent approaches to dealing with the bullying as well as ways to avoid situations both in and out of school where bullying is likely to occur. If bullying persists, keep a written record, and determine if the police should be involved after exploring the issue with school personnel.

As a parent, your behavior strongly influences your child. Children reflect the ways of their parents. Be a good role model, and monitor your own aggressive behavior. Reevaluate how you discipline your children. Nonviolent approaches to discipline teach children to deal with others in nonviolent ways. Be aware of what triggers aggression in your child, and discuss alternatives that are peaceful and diplomatic. Reward appropriate and tactful behaviors, and discourage behaviors that are hostile and destructive.

Suggest ways your child can be of service to others rather than to be cruel to them. Volunteering at a local hospital or nursing home, offering to read to younger children at a local library, and helping elderly neighbors with chores are a few ways to build self-esteem. When youngsters feel good about themselves, they are less likely to engage in bullying.

Parents have the responsibility of monitoring their children's actions and behavior and holding them accountable for hurtful actions toward others. Violent actions and bullying cannot be tolerated. Parents must instill strong values and respect for others. When children violate others, it is the parents' job to step in and make their children answerable to the victims they abuse. Finally, teach them proper behaviors that promote kindness and toleration toward others who may be different.

SUGGESTIONS FOR STUDENTS

All students have the right to feel safe and secure. This includes traveling to and from school, within the school building, and within outdoor areas surrounding the school such as playgrounds and athletic fields. Most students will encounter a situation involving a bully during their school career. It may involve teasing or name-calling, or it may involve something more severe like a physical altercation. During these incidents, students may assume the role of victim, bystander, or bully. Regardless of the situation, bullying is harmful and can have long-lasting effects on young people.

If you fall victim to a bully, there are some strategies you can use to handle yourself and possibly avoid the altercation altogether. Here are some worth trying:

- If a bully approaches you, stand tall and make eye contact. Using a firm tone of voice, make statements like, "Leave me alone" or "Stop picking on me."
- Try not to cry or appear afraid.

- Walk away from the bully.
- Spend time with friends, and travel with a group because bullies tend to avoid bothering individuals who are part of a group and not alone.
- Report any incident involving bullying to an adult you can trust.
  - A parent, teacher, faculty member, or principal are good choices.
- If you have difficulty verbalizing your thoughts and feelings, write them down.
  - This is especially helpful if the bullying is ongoing. Documents will help substantiate your case. You can give your written statement to a trusted adult who can help you. You should keep a copy for yourself.
- Use humor in the face of a bully. Make a joke about yourself.
  - This could distract the bully away from the situation and become less interested in picking on you.

If you are a bystander who witnesses acts of bullying, there are some steps you can take to help the victim and prevent further incidents from occurring. Here is what you can do:

- Be supportive to the victim, and walk away from the bully together.
- If you know someone who is bullied, be a friend, and extend an invitation to do things with you and your peer group.
- Help someone who is being bullied by gathering a group of your friends together to verbalize a message to the bully that bullying is wrong.
- If you have a friend who bullies others, tell that person to stop and suggest seeking out an adult who can help your friend deal with this problem. Let the bully know you are confident he or she can change for the better.
- Report all bully-related incidents to a trusted adult.
- Never do nothing because this condones bullying and indicates you think bullying is okay.

Bullying is a serious offense. If you are a bully and continue to harass others, you will remain on a path that will ultimately lead to negative repercussions. Eventually, you will be held accountable for your actions. The consequences may even extend beyond the school and involve the law. Here is what you can do to take a look at yourself and change your behavior:

- Adopt the belief that no one has the right to hurt someone else.
- Adopt the belief that bullying is wrong at any age.
- Learn about the harmful effects of bullying. Take part in ant-bullying activities.
- Join a support group for bullies.
- Seek help. Consider one-on-one counseling with an expert. Consider peer counseling.

- Consider mediation if your problem is with one particular individual.
- Start treating others the way you want to be treated.
- Be aware of the thoughts and feelings that trigger your bullying. Learn and practice strategies that help you maintain self-control.
- Be aware of the effects your bullying has on others.
- Participate in activities that you are good at and make you feel good about yourself.
- Become responsible for your actions, and accept the consequences you deserve. Then make a commitment to yourself that you will change for the better.

Situations involving bullying are growing in number. The best ways for young people to protect themselves are to understand the motives of bullies, the consequences for wrongdoings, and the actions that can be taken to prevent further incidents from occurring. Every incident involving bullying should not be ignored. Every incident involving bullying should be reported to someone who has the authority to act on it.

Cyberbullying

The Internet has made it possible for yet another type of bullying to emerge. It is perhaps the most dangerous of all forms of bullying because the scope of this kind of bullying is far-reaching both in the tactics used and the number of individuals affected. The plotting and the scheming of cyberbullies seem to intensify every day. A portion of this chapter has been devoted to addressing cyberbullying because it is a growing problem in schools and homes everywhere. Here is what educators, parents, and students need to know.

Cyberbullying occurs among children, preteens, and teens. Generally, it is bullying through the use of the Internet, digital technologies, and mobile phones. The line of attack chosen to bully in this way depends upon the cyberbully's thoughts, imagination, level of technology, and access to technology.

Cyberbullying can escalate and get out of hand very quickly. It is a problem that cannot be ignored. Here is the proof. Among six- to eleven-year-olds, 17 percent reported that they received threats or embarrassing material through e-mails, instant messages, websites, chat rooms, or text messages. The statistics jump to 36 percent among 12- to 17-year-olds.

Preteens say they are bullied at school 45 percent of the time and bullied at home 45 percent of the time. Teens report being bullied at school 30 percent of the time and bullied at home 70 percent of the time. Girls are victims or perpetrators of cyberbullying twice as much as boys are. Boys tend to gravitate more toward physical forms of aggression as bullies.

The role of bully and victim can vacillate. An individual may assume the role of bully at one point and the role of victim at another. Cyberbullying is limited to minors. When adults bully through technology, it is not considered cyberbullying. Rather it is called cyberharassment or cyberstalking.

Two types of cyberbullying exist: direct attacks and indirect attacks. Direct attacks occur when the victim receives messages directly. These are some examples of direct attacks:

- Instant messaging
- Stealing passwords
- Creating blogs that damage another individual's reputation or invades someone's privacy
- Creating websites meant to insult or endanger an individual by posting personal information or degrading photographs
- Sending degrading pictures through e-mails and cell phones
- Internet polling by asking questions that generate answers meant to damage the character or reputation of another
- Interactive gaming that allows youngsters to communicate by chat and live Internet phone with people they are matched up with in an online game
  - Interactive gaming allows a cyberbully to lock others out of games, spread rumors, make threats, or hack into various accounts.
- Sending harmful codes such as viruses and software to victims and hacking programs
- Sending pornography, junk e-mail, and IMs
  - Cyberbullies can place their victims on IM marketing lists and sign them up to receive e-mails that can be pornographic in nature.
- Impersonation
  - By assuming a victim's identity, a cyberbully may post inappropriate messages in a hate group's chat room while volunteering the victim's personal contact information, making the victim an easy target for many others.
- Hacking into accounts, stealing passwords, and setting up new accounts while pretending to be the victim
- Using chat rooms where inappropriate messages can appear on the screens of those who are signed in
- Using cell phones to send text messages, call, and verbally bully another individual, or leave voicemail messages that may be hurtful in nature or as a form of harassment

In general, a cyberbully's motive is to hurt or embarrass others. Many factors prompt this kind of a bully to injure others using technology for self-satisfaction. Cyberbullies pursue victims for the following reasons:

- Feelings of anger and the desire to seek revenge
- Entertainment
  - Many cyberbullies have a wide variety of technology toys at their disposal, but choose to use them in destructive ways.
- The joy of attaining a reaction from others
- Boosting ego
- Revenge on individuals who defend others in the face of injustice
- Enjoyment from engaging in secretive operations
- Recognition gained from an audience
- Desire for power
  - Many cyberbullies view themselves as weak individuals both in character and in stature. Technology may be their only strength.

A high degree of technology skills make cyberbullies the most dangerous bullies of all. Encourage young people to take a stand against cyberbullying. Education is beneficial. Children and teens need to know how easy it is to fall victim to a cyberbully, and the effects can be long-term and difficult to rectify. Provide them with the means to protect themselves. Cyberbullies, on the other hand, need to be aware of the consequences for their actions. It should be stressed that cyberbullying is a criminal offense, involving law enforcement in many cases and even the FBI in serious cases.

Our twenty-first century children and teens have lived with technology from the start of their schooling. They quickly become proficient in skills that many of their teachers and parents lack. Still, they may be unaware of the ramifications of the improper use of technology to harm others. They may be ignorant of the aspects of cyberbullying and its harmful effects. Share information on the causes, dangerous effects, and consequences of cyberbullying. Offer opportunities for students to report incidents of cyberbullying anonymously in school. Tell them how to go about reporting incidents that occur outside of the school. Young people are the most effective helpers in combating cyberbullying.

Regardless of age, it is important for children and teens to recognize when they are being threatened and to determine the degree of seriousness. Encourage them to keep track of the frequency in which threats occur. Threats can take on many forms, but, in terms of cyberbullying, they often appear as messages. What does a threatening message contain? The following list will offer some possible answers:

- Crude and vulgar language
- Insults
- Vague threats

- Threats of bodily harm
- Threats that may affect the general public, such as a bomb scare
- Threats of serious bodily harm or death

A threat may be a one-time occurrence. It can be repeated in the same or different way. It can increase in number, and it can involve additional people. A threat can be made by:

- A person the child or teen knows
- A person the child or teen does not know
- A person the child or teen thinks he or she knows

A threat may even come from several different people. Consider the following examples to be threatening in nature:

- E-mails or IMs that occur repeatedly
- Following a young person around online to locations such as chat rooms or websites
- Creating false profiles, websites, e-mails, or IMs while assuming the identity of the victim
- Breaking into the victim's online accounts or stealing passwords
- Sharing the victim's personal, intimate, or contact information
- Impersonating a child or teen for any purpose
- Posting real or altered images, sexual or nonsexual, of a young person online
- Adding a child or teen to an online list such as a hit list

With increased use of the Internet, opportunities for sharing and posting personal information have grown. The ramifications of having personal information available online has become very serious, creating more possibilities for identity theft. If the personal information of a child under the age of 13 is posted online, the website or Internet service provider is required under the Children's Online Privacy Protection Act (COPPA) to remove the information at once.

Cyberstalkers and harassers often use the Internet to post sexual want ads and solicit adults and young people. Posting personal information makes it easier for perpetrators to attain victims. If a child or teen is targeted, alert the Internet service provider, and involve law enforcement agents.

Parents should always be accessible to their children and teens. They need to be approachable and remain nonjudgmental in situations involving all kinds of bullying. Children and teens are also reluctant to share incidents involving cyberbullying with their parents just as they are with other forms of bullying. Parents, therefore, must be vigilant when it comes to computer use. Placing the computer in an open area will help.

Watch for signs of cyberbullying such as upsetting behavior after using the computer or receiving a text message, withdrawal from social activities and interactions, and a sudden unexplained decline in school grades and performance.

When a young person becomes the victim of cyberbullying, parents are urged to assess the severity of the situation. Determine if the child or teen is at risk for physical harm or assault as well as the emotional effects resulting from the involvement. Document all possible evidence. Then contact authorities that can provide advice and assistance. The local law enforcement agency, the Internet service provider, and the school are practical starting points.

As a result of recent legislation, many states require or encourage officials to address forms of school bullying. Arkansas, Florida, Idaho, Iowa, Kentucky, Maryland, Missouri, Rhode Island, South Carolina, and Washington require schools to specifically deal with matters involving cyberbullying.

Parents need to keep the lines of communication open. Openly talking about cyberbullying and its harmful effects on the bully and the victim is important. Children and teens should be encouraged to go to their parents if they are being cyberbullied. Parents should reassure them that they will not lose computer privileges if they are involved in cyberbullying in some way.

Parents can also teach their youngsters some precautions that will keep them safe and decrease the chances of becoming an injured party of cyberbullying. These safeguards are worth sharing with children and teens:

- Never give out an e-mail password or any password that would allow a cyberbully access to personal information.
- Choose passwords that are difficult for others to figure out.
- Do not open e-mails from bullies or strangers.
- Save and show parents messages from cyberbullies, and do not respond to them.
- Never share personal information on the Internet or share information or pictures other people should not see.
- Avoid visiting inappropriate sites.
- Refrain from sending e-mails, texting, or responding to others when angry.

Cyberbullying is a dangerous practice and should be taken seriously. Parents and educators are cautioned to watch for signs at home and at school so bullies can be confronted. Although cyberbullying cannot be avoided, educators, parents, and students can join forces to prevent it from becoming stronger and harming greater numbers of young people.

School districts typically establish an acceptable computer use policy as a safety measure to prevent students from engaging in harmful cyber practices or becoming the recipient of harmful cyber practices. It should be strongly enforced by schools. Parents and students should be required to sign the policy as a commitment to abide by its rules. Schools have a responsibility to ensure its students understand the privileges that occur when using a school's computers as well as the consequences that occur when violating their use. The policy should also dictate the specific consequences that accompany cyberbullying.

Most school districts install filters as safeguards to prevent students from accessing harmful or inappropriate information, ads, websites, or sexually explicit places on the Internet where young people tend to gravitate. Once in place, these filters will sort appropriate and inappropriate Internet locations. They enforce Internet usage policies by blocking access to Internet sites that are improper and not school-related. Such filters even restrict personal web browsing for educators and students.

Bullying is everybody's business. Educators and parents must make a commitment to become involved when bully-related issues arise. Forming a partnership between educators and parents enables them to meet this challenge effectively by reinforcing the same message. When educators and parents send a clear and consistent message that bullying is wrong and serve as strong role models who reject all forms of bullying, young people will recognize the importance of toleration and interact respectfully within the school environment and beyond.

Chapter 8

Promoting Good Decision-Making

Decision-making ability is needed to function in today's society. It is a valuable and important skill because the decisions that children make will impact their lives greatly. Good decisions result in satisfaction and self-fulfillment. Poor decisions provide learning experiences that affect their future. This chapter is designed to make educators, parents, and students aware of how powerful decision-making can impact the lives of individuals. It also serves to provide information and suggestions for handling issues such as substance abuse, peer pressure, and Internet safety.

ESSENTIALS FOR EDUCATORS

Historically, scientists believed the human brain essentially forms during childhood. New research has revealed that the brain undergoes radical changes during adolescence. Physical movement, vision, and the senses develop first in the brain while the frontal portions of the brain that control higher-level thinking are not fully developed until an individual reaches his or her early twenties and sometimes later in men. This developmental process could place teens at a higher risk for making some decisions that will be regretted later.

While the prefrontal cortex responsible for assessing risks and rewards develops later, the limbic system matures earlier. This system controls emotions. The lag in these stages of brain development could explain why teens more often follow their hearts and not their heads. They hastily make decisions that may result in consequences that affect their health or place them in situations involving the legal system. Engaging in drug or alcohol use,

91

stealing, or sexual activity are behaviors that involve poor decision-making and result in harmful long-term consequences.

Throughout childhood and adolescence, the brain experiences two processes: myelination and synaptic pruning. These processes increase the brain's efficiency and shape it according to a person's experiences and activities. The kinds of experiences and activities that children. and especially teens, are involved in are important. Teens ultimately have the potential to mold their own brain development through the choices they make and the behaviors they exhibit.

Brains require plenty of sleep. Nine hours and fifteen minutes of sleep each night is necessary, especially for adolescents, for proper functioning in school. During sleep time, brains consolidate memory. Brains also require a great deal of energy. A diet of well-balanced, healthy food beginning with breakfast is essential to replenish energy. Drug and alcohol use should be avoided. Such substances are harmful to long- and short-term memory and lead to addiction faster than in adults.

It was once thought that adolescents operated the way adults did when they used reasoning as a basis for the decisions they made. It is now believed that adolescent decisions are not planned, but rather are reactions to circumstances that usually involve peers and friends. Personal and social images of themselves are usually what steers them toward risky impulsive behaviors. The need for portraying a particular image among peers is strong.

Studies indicate that one of the most influential factors for inhibiting behaviors that lead to serious outcomes is spending time with a responsible adult. Monitoring teen behavior is also essential at this time. Effective thinking skills, responsibility, and strengthening the ability to weigh consequences can be achieved through a relationship with good rapport between the adult and the teen. Parents and educators may be more successful communicating with adolescents by sharing how they, as adults, are feeling rather than using dominating word choices.

Because the regions of the brain are not in balance, teens will require more guidance. The adolescent brain is built to learn. Providing opportunities that build good physical skills, learning skills, creativity, and decision-making ability are crucial for effective brain development. Providing information to teens on how the brain works along with activities that encourage smart choices, thinking before asking, and evaluating positive and negative consequences of decisions are most helpful in guiding and keeping adolescents on the right path.

In order for students to succeed in school, they need to make appropriate choices both in and out of school. Educators can set the tone for student success and, at the same time, teach students how their decisions will impact their future. Whenever possible, involve students in decision-making processes that affect the course of study. Serve as a model for them to illustrate how to weigh the consequences of decisions.

Provide role-playing opportunities for real-world problems involving decision-making and the identification of positive and negative consequences. The frontal lobe of the brain is responsible for memory. Memory ability enhances during adolescence. This is an excellent time for educators to incorporate communication skills, debating opportunities, cooperative grouping, and oral presentations into instruction. Movement throughout a class period and the school day increases memory. Because memory and decision-making ability are linked, any opportunity for bodily motion is helpful to students.

Schools and classrooms typically operate under an agreed-upon set of rules and expectations. When developing such rules and expectations, committees consisting of major stakeholders are usually formed to establish them. Be sure that students are a part of these committees if they are age-appropriate. Establishing classroom rules and expectations can work the same way. Generate meaningful discussions to acquire students' ideas and perceptions of how the class should function. Students are more likely to take ownership and follow what is established if they have been a part of the decision-making process.

Choose classroom goals, rules, and expectations that are realistic and meaningful to students to enhance understanding and ownership. Provide a rationale to justify their need. Engage students in a discussion to determine potential problems that may arise once they are in place. This type of decision-making process allows students to feel like a greater part of the school and classroom community. Post goals, rules, and expectations in a visually prominent place. Review them on a regular basis to evaluate their effectiveness.

Educators are in a key position to support healthy adolescent growth. Understanding the teen brain and the biological changes that adolescents go through will place educators in a better position to provide their students with realistic, meaningful experiences and interventions.

As students reach the age of maturity, or puberty, certain hormonal changes occur that can influence the way they make decisions. Boys who enter puberty at an early age may exhibit higher self-esteem and cognitive functioning. They often associate with an older group of peers and experience greater popularity. They are more likely to make decisions that involve risky behavior.

Like their male counterparts, girls who enter puberty at an early age are also more likely to make decisions involving risky behavior. Their motives are based more upon lower self-esteem, anxiety, and depression. These feelings can provoke girls to engage in risk-taking behaviors involving sexual activity and eating disorders.

Providing students with a framework for support that involves school personnel, parents, and outside resources when needed can reduce harmful behaviors. This is especially true for individuals with histories of risk-taking behaviors. This type of intervention can also make a difference for students who are considering engaging in harmful behaviors.

All students need to know that there are adults available whom they can turn to for advice and direction. It is important for those who are directly involved with high-risk teens to collaborate regularly. Students need an availability of activities that build upon their strengths as well as effective problem-solving strategies that keep them from a path of destruction.

The brain's volume increases. Its ability to make connections nearly doubles, leading to large amounts of experimentation between the ages of 11 and 25 as adolescents search for an identity. They often separate from parents emotionally and believe they are invincible. Educators and parents need to be mindful of this time in a young adult's life.

Educators can provide the guidance needed for teens to learn to reflect on their own behavior, whether it is good or bad. Time is needed for teens to reflect on the choices they have made and take responsibility for them. They need to learn to feel proud of good choices and to acknowledge mistakes rather than place blame on others. Accepting the consequence and learning from mistakes is essential so poor decisions will not be repeated. Help adolescents to believe that everyone makes mistakes and to forgive themselves for wrongdoings.

In order to assist parents in developing an understanding of their child or adolescent, design and hold parenting classes to educate parents on developmental issues. Help parents to see the importance of shifting more control to adolescents in terms of accepting more responsibility for their actions, learning from their mistakes, and seeing the benefit of weighing consequences. Partnerships among educators, parents, and students have proven to aid students in developing a sense of self and accepting more personal and social responsibility.

While adolescents struggle to determine a sense of self, they also crave a sense of belonging. The need to be listened to, and the need for contributing are important to them. Opportunities where students can formulate their own questions for inquiry, design and conduct an investigation, and draw conclusions from their findings can fulfill these needs. Such situations, both in and out of school, encourage these individuals to think critically, speak up for themselves, and voice their opinions. These skills reinforce decision-making ability.

Currently, a strong interest in protecting the environment exists. Today's young people are in a pivotal position to make responsible decisions that will impact the fate of our planet. Many students are aware of environmental issues, but lack the knowledge to motivate them to be a part of the solution.

The work of Mike Weilbacher, director of the Lower Merion Conservatory in Gladwyne, Pennsylvania, has been successful in educating young people about environmental issues. He travels the United States as an environmental educator, performer, and workshop presenter. He has studied the educational benefits of immersing students in the outdoors and environmental education experiences. He developed a model that includes a list of concepts that every student should know about the environment. He suggests that educators cover the concepts suggested in the list as students move from kindergarten to high school.

The list of concepts is vital to environmental education, and permission was granted to share it with readers. By addressing these concepts, students will receive a heightened awareness and be better equipped to make many more environmentally correct decisions. It is as follows:

1. Earth overflows with life.
   * One of science's biggest mysteries is how many species share this planet—estimates range from 5 million to 100 million species. Many environmental education programs begin with the premise that life is vanishing; young learners should know that Earth teems with a huge number of creatures.
2. Each creature is uniquely adapted to its environment.
   * Every species evolved to possess a unique set of adaptations that enables it to survive and thrive in its ecosystem. Students should be on a first name basis with many local creatures.
3. The web of life is interdependent.
   * Organisms evolve complex relationships, each depending on numerous other species for their survival.
4. Materials flow through ecosystems in cycles.
   * All creatures need water, air, and nutrients to survive. These materials cycle and recycle through ecosystems. The water we drink today is the same water we've always had, and always will.
5. The sun is the ultimate source of energy flowing through ecosystems.
   * Food grows from sunlight energy; our houses are heated by fossil fuels created many millennia ago from ancient sunlight.
6. There is no waste in nature; everything is recycled.
   * In nature, every waste product is used by other creatures. Humans have bent those circles into straight lines, where things are used once and tossed.

7. We consume resources to live.
   • Every student should know where the trash truck takes the trash, where water comes from, and how the nearest power plant makes electricity.
8. Conservation is the wise use of finite resources.
   • We are physical creatures with real needs—to eat, drink, build houses, write on paper. But how do we use these resources sustainably?
9. Humans can have a profound effect on environmental systems.
   • Fossil fuels pump carbon dioxide into the sky; habitat loss is causing the extinction of large numbers of species. Our actions profoundly affect the ecological systems that sustain living things—and us. Nature can often repair these systems (forests grow back, for example; but humans are changing systems faster than nature can adapt).
10. Each of us can powerfully affect the fate of the natural world.
   • Because each of us is directly plugged into the planet, the actions we take—or fail to take—profoundly influence earth's systems.

Schools teach what they consider to be important to make students productive and responsible citizens. With global warming, an explosion in population growth, and the expending of resources, educators must produce students who are environmentally literate enough to make decisions that will benefit mankind.

Education includes many facets. Today, schools are not only responsible for the academic success of their students, but also for their moral character and social responsibility. Ethical and socially responsible students are likely to make healthy decisions that involve themselves and others.

Factors such as peers, genetic influences, and different forms of media affect students' moral development. Parents, however, play the greatest role in influencing moral character. Parents either cultivate or undermine elements of kindness, honesty, courage, moral reasoning, and a sense of justice and responsibility for others. These attributes influence the kinds of decisions that young people will make. Establishing a strong relationship among parents, students, and educators are crucial for a student's healthy moral character.

Adults who interact with children and adolescents need to assess their own values before imposing them on others. Educators and parents must agree on the common values they want to instill in young people and create an ethical environment at school and at home.

In situations involving high-risk students with hard-to-reach parents, it is essential for educators to find a way to get parents on board and work together to address the problematic behavior. Without parental support, it will be difficult to change the behavior in a positive way. Acknowledge diversity, and recognize the contributions the student could make to the school community and the community in which he or she lives. Foster the educator-parent relationship by encouraging the word "we" and not "I" when discussing the student. Invite parents to share their ideas about what may work to address the problematic behavior and to commit to taking a role in the solution.

PRACTICES FOR PARENTS

One of the most significant things that parents can do to shape their children into individuals who are happy and successful is to teach them good decision-making skills. Then permit them to make their own decisions whenever possible. In addition, children who make good decisions become adults who make valuable contributions to society.

Parents need to begin teaching good decision-making at an early age. Children often act without thinking. Teach them how to think a decision through. For very young children, offer a limited amount of choices to make and let them decide on the one that best suits them. As children become older, increase the number of options they have to choose from before allowing them to select one. Always try to help them to determine the positive and negative consequences of their decisions, also known as weighing the pros and cons. Encourage them to do this every time they are faced with making a decision.

When your child or adolescent makes a decision, evaluate it. Why was the decision a good one? Why was the decision a poor one? If the decision was a poor one, hold your child responsible for his or her actions. Allow your child to learn from his or her mistakes by pondering the results. Assess how the results affected others. Assess how the results affected your child. Finally, determine if the decision was the best one possible for the situation. This will help your child to ultimately make better decisions in the future.

Using imaginary situations to teach decision-making to children can be helpful. Consider using children's literature. It is not only fun to read it together, but it also presents actions and consequences that are understandable.

Children's literature is also effective when teaching right from wrong, and many stories are filled with content that promotes good character traits. Some especially effective stories suggested by expert Pamela Leong include *The Ants and the Grasshopper, The Little Red Hen, The Three Little Kittens, The Tortoise and the Hare,* and *Pinocchio.* Think about selecting stories that match family values.

Situations involving problems facing adolescents can be used more with teens. Family discussions that center on subjects like peer pressure, drug and alcohol abuse, sexual activity, smoking, drunk driving, and eating disorders should take place on a regular basis. These issues lend themselves to teaching the positive and negative consequences that can result from the kinds of decisions made surrounding them.

Adolescence can be a painful growing time for both parents and teens. It is also an important time when preteens and teens experience huge physical and emotional changes. Parents may have to work even harder at this level to teach good decision-making skills that will help their adolescents grow into the unique individuals they will become.

Many young people indicate they are entering into adolescence by displaying a dramatic change in behavior. They begin to distance themselves from their parents. They strive for independence. They care about how others perceive them, and they try desperately to fit in. Adolescents often begin to experiment with new looks and identities that can cause conflict with their parents.

There is no trouble-free solution for parents to get through those difficult years of adolescence, but there are some ways to make the journey smoother. Begin by educating yourself on the adolescent years. Read books, journal articles, or information recommended by experts in the field or provided by credible adolescent websites.

Learn about the physical and emotional changes teens go through. Learn about the behaviors to expect, the mood changes, and the possible conflicts between parent and teen. Be aware of the pressures that teens may face. Not every teen faces adolescence in the same way. Parents who are aware of what to expect during those years are in a better position to help their teen, and they are able to cope better themselves.

Informing your teen about what to expect during adolescence is equally important. Discussing sex, drugs, alcohol, and tobacco use before your teen is exposed will make him or her better prepared to act responsibly when confronted by them. This is also a good time to discuss peer pressure with your youngster and the harmful consequences that can result from giving in to it. Know your teen's friends. Know where your teen is as well as the activities he or she participates in. For safety reasons, parents should always know where their teen is going, what he or she is doing, and whom he or she is doing it with.

Monitor what your teen watches and reads. Know what your teen is reading and learning from the media. Set limits on television and computer use, especially when it concerns the Internet. Internet content and contacts made through the Internet can be especially dangerous.

Communicate in a nonthreatening way. Adolescents will not respond positively when they feel like they are being watched. Respect their sense of privacy whenever possible. As teens move into young adulthood, they will need to experience some privacy. Parents, however, need to mindful of situations when it is safe to do so.

Educating yourself about adolescence and staying informed means you are likely to recognize the warning signs that signal your teen could be in trouble. Parents are cautioned to be on their guard for the following warning signs:

- Excessive weight loss or gain
- Problems sleeping
- Quick and dramatic changes in personality
- Continuously avoiding school or excessive absenteeism
- Failing grades
- Suicidal thoughts or comments
- Signs of tobacco, alcohol, or drug use
- Trouble with the law

If any of these behaviors persist, consult your doctor, a school or outside counselor or psychologist, or a psychiatrist.

Talk with your teen about his or her concerns. Answer his or her questions, especially those that relate to his or her body. Provide books and other resources on puberty. Share your own experiences about adolescence and puberty. Open the lines of communication early, and keep them open. Be aware that your teen may be self-conscious about certain issues he or she experiences. Show empathy for his or her feelings.

Develop house rules and high expectations for good grades and behavior, and stick to them. Be sure the rules and expectations are realistic and attainable. For example, bedtimes and curfews should be age-appropriate. If parents have appropriate rules and expectations, teens are likely to attempt to meet them. Teens should be rewarded for compliance and demonstrating they are trustworthy individuals.

When teens falter, pick your battles with them. If the behavior is inappropriate but harmless, allow it to happen without significant reprimand or punishment. Seriously object, however, to behavior involving things like school failure, sex, alcohol, drugs, smoking, or stealing.

The lives of millions of adolescents are currently affected by the increasing use of drugs and alcohol. Among 12- to 17-year-olds, 9.3 percent are illicit drug users. Within the age group of 18 to 25, illicit drug use nearly doubles to 19.6 percent.

Statistics further reveal that among Americans aged 12 or older, 51.6 percent are current drinkers of alcohol with 57.7 percent being male, and 49.9 percent being female. The data can be further broken down to show a steady increase in current alcohol use as age increases.

- 3.4 percent of 12- and 13-year-olds currently drink alcohol
- 13.1 percent of 14- and 15-year-olds currently drink alcohol
- 26.2 percent of 16- and 17-year-olds currently drink alcohol
- 48.7 percent of 18- and 20-year-olds currently drink alcohol
- 69.5 percent of 21- and 25-year-olds currently drink alcohol
  (National Household Survey on Drug Abuse 2008).

Adolescents are confronted with serious risks associated with substance abuse. These risks often result in harmful consequences. Traffic accidents top the list. School-related problems involving failing grades, excessive absenteeism, and dropping out can result. Engaging in sexual practices that lead to unplanned pregnancies and sexually transmitted diseases are more likely to happen. Delinquent behavior such as running away from home, stealing, fighting, or attacking others can occur. Juvenile crimes involving the sale of drugs, the use of a handgun, and the association with a gang escalates.

The ramifications of substance abuse are endless. Developmental problems that affect an adolescent's psychological and social development increase. Physical and mental states are also affected. Marijuana use in particular can impair short-term memory, comprehension, one's sense of time, and the ability to maintain coordination. Early alcohol use has been linked to alcohol dependence later in life.

Parents should be aware of these warning signs. These behaviors could indicate a substance abuse problem:

- Sudden, unexplainable personality changes
- Loss of interest in one's favorite pastimes, sports, or other activities
- Sudden change in grades at school
- Increased absenteeism at school or work
- Changes in friendships or an unwillingness to talk about new friendships
- A disheveled appearance or lack of interest in personal grooming habits
- Difficulty paying attention in and out of school or forgetfulness
- Unexpected changes in behavior such as aggressiveness, irritability, nervousness, or giddiness
- Secretive behavior and responding to questions in a highly sensitive manner (Center for Substance Abuse Treatment 1999)

If a parent suspects that his or her teen is involved in some type of substance abuse, a number of interventions can be pursued. Tackle the problem as a family. The substance abuse problem can sometimes be a result of a family issue. Parents need to be a part of the entire treatment process.

Utilize school resources. A school nurse, guidance counselor, or school psychologist, social worker, or substance abuse coordinator can provide valuable information for a family and counseling for the teen. If a teen requires a more serious path of treatment, parents may have to consider the services of a physician, hospital, or mental health facility. Substance abuse support groups for teens and their families are often available through the school, church, or hospital and are yet another avenue for parents to pursue.

Other problematic behaviors that occur during adolescence include stealing, fighting, sexual activity, and truancy. These behaviors can be associated with the type of friends that an adolescent has. Adolescents are less likely to participate in such behaviors when they have friends who do well in school, actively participate in school activities, are mentally healthy, and do not engage in harmful substances such as tobacco, drugs, or alcohol.

The goals and beliefs of the school also play a role in helping to shape students' character development and decision-making ability. Students who exhibit problematic behavior are often associated with peers who are in direct opposition to the school's mission. Problematic behavior is also associated with the amount of time that peers spend with each other and whether or not these individuals fit in at school.

During adolescence, teens are greatly influenced by their peers. They tend to spend more time with peers and less time with family. Parents must be aware of the peer relationships that their adolescents are involved in. Assist them in choosing friends who have similar interests and values held by your own family. Things like academic success, respect for self and others, and an avoidance of harmful substances are critical and should be shared by the friends your adolescent is involved with.

Your teen should feel loved and supported by family and friends. This will increase self-esteem and self-worth. These feelings build the confidence needed to avoid associating with inappropriate friends and becoming involved in harmful situations. Always recognize and praise good decision-making in the presence of peer pressure.

Talk with your teen as soon as you observe behavior that was negatively influenced by peers. Discuss the consequences of such behavior. Discourage association with inappropriate peers. Together, discuss ways to handle the situation. If you are unable to resolve the problem, seek out professionals who can assist you.

Monitor and control negative influences on your teen, such as television, video games, books, magazines, and the Internet. Your teen may choose and use these sources inappropriately on his or her own, or his or her choices may be a result of recommendations made by a peer. Today's use of the Internet can be harmful to an unsuspecting teen. Numerous opportunities exist for teens to form dangerous relationships. Parents will want to ensure that their youngster, regardless of age, does not fall victim to an Internet crime.

Parents can monitor computer use by installing the computers that children and teens use in a common family area. Create a list of agreed-upon family computer rules. Hang these rules where they can be easily seen and reviewed often. Develop a family computer use schedule that is fair for all members. Be sure that computer time is not abused so it does not interfere with family time, schoolwork, friends, or other activities.

Teach your child or teen to distinguish between safe and unsafe Internet relationships. Frequently discuss information that should never be shared over the Internet. Stress how sharing personal information could be used to locate an individual by a perpetrator. The following list includes information that should never be shared:

- Age
- Sex
- Location
- School name
- Grade
- Date of birth
- Name
- Nickname
- Address
- Home telephone number
- Cell phone number
- Graduating class
- Sports played
- Sports team name

This kind of personal information should never be shared. In fact, children and adolescents should not converse with anyone they do not know through the computer. Always insist on using a secure password not to be shared with anyone. Be sure that your child or adolescent is careful about what he or she posts online and he or she only goes to sites you know are safe. Ask your child to refrain from clicking on pop-ups and to never put pictures of himself or herself online. Finally, encourage your child to report if he or she is cyberbullied to you or another responsible adult.

You can further ensure your youngster's safety by routinely checking computer activity. Examine history files, unfamiliar bookmarked sites, documents, cookies, and trashed items. Be watchful for signs of secrecy, excessive amounts of time spent using the computer, and unauthorized e-mail accounts. Consider making use of blocking, filtering, or monitoring controls on the computer. Lastly, attend Internet safety classes for families offered by schools, the town, or city in which you live. They are conducted by experts who remain up-to-date on the best practices for proper and safe Internet use.

Our children and teens are faced with making decisions on a daily basis. While we cannot always expect them to make the best decisions possible, we can at least provide them with a solid foundation that includes recognizing positive and negative consequences beginning at an early age. It is the ultimate goal of parents and educators alike to form partnerships that will produce individuals who will grow into adults whose decisions result in healthy and productive contributions to society.

Chapter 9

Fostering Independence and Improving Reading through Everyday Activities

Children who are independent readers have mastered basic reading skills and can usually teach themselves new things through reading. Research shows that the more children read, the more their skills improve. Independent readers are also independent thinkers and can respond to what they read.

In order for children to become independent readers, educators must find ways to involve parents in the process. Children will not be motivated to read unless parents believe reading is a vital and important skill that extends beyond the school day.

This chapter is designed to supply educators with information to use to build partnerships with parents who recognize the significance of reading and promote independent reading through the means of a family literacy night.

This chapter will also furnish parents with tips to nurture a growing reader and foster independence through reading. Everyday activities will be shared to strengthen reading skills that will, in turn, also cultivate independence.

Summer reading influences reading achievement. Information will be provided about its impact as well as ways for parents to encourage summer reading and show that reading is a year-round activity. These activities and suggestions will help to keep reading skills current. They also serve as a vehicle to bring families together to share in worthwhile experiences that reinforce education.

ESSENTIALS FOR EDUCATORS

Educators are faced with the challenge of motivating children to read. With rigorous government mandates and unique family structures, more than ever, this challenge is perhaps greater to overcome. Without family support in the area of reading, an educator's role can become increasingly difficult to fulfill.

Educators are faced with a difficult task, and one way to accomplish what is needed is to bring educators and families together for a family literacy night. A family literacy night can typically involve:

- Educators
- Students
- Parents
- Guardians
- Family members such as siblings, grandparents, aunts, and uncles
- Any other responsible adults who interact with the children in the school

Begin by securing a date that accommodates the attendees' schedules and a location to house a large group of individuals. Allow space for presentations, displays, and refreshments. Enlist students, and assign them the responsibility of designing, writing, and sending invitations to the appropriate guests. Advertise the event in parent newsletters, school and local newspapers, and on the school website.

Conduct the family literacy night within a reasonable time frame of no more than two to three hours to make the event manageable for staff members and families. Consider the audience when establishing the start and ending times as well as when determining the structure and content of the event.

Identify valuable reading skills, and create learning centers that explain the instructional strategies and approaches teachers are utilizing in their classrooms. Invite teachers to model lessons while stationed at the learning centers. Provide handouts with helpful hints for parents. They can bring these suggestions home and use them when working with their children.

Create activities that offer opportunities for sharing. Family reading circles where books are available for family members to read to one another and game centers where teachers, students, and parents can create games that teach about letters and words are examples. Encourage parents to bring photos and mementos to share and complement a family story or history.

Parents and family members enjoy viewing products of their children's work as well as watching their children perform in some manner. Design a program where students can share a book through a read-aloud, sing a song, recite a poem, or participate in a short skit.

Invite local authors and storytellers to attend the event. They may be willing to volunteer their time for such a worthwhile cause.

Consider holding a book swap during a family literacy night. It is inexpensive and a great way to make room in a home library for books of interest acquired from the swap.

Finally, provide refreshments for all participants and small gifts for the parents who attend. Solicit local restaurants, supermarkets, businesses, and bookstores for donations. Have students write follow-up thank you notes for the donations. Publicize the success of the family literacy night in school newspapers or newsletters, local newspapers, and on the school website. Better yet, make the family literacy night a yearly event.

PRACTICES FOR PARENTS

Family functioning influences reading at all grade levels. When families read and write themselves, it shows that literacy is valued, and children and adolescents are likely to follow the example. Families that engage in verbal interaction allow children and adolescents opportunities to form and express their ideas and opinions. Reading together as a family and discussing the printed word contributes to making children and adolescents literate. A wide range of reading materials available in the home will assure that literacy experiences can occur. When parents have high expectations, children and adolescents are more likely to hold them for themselves and become literate beings.

Literacy starts at a very early age. It is important to begin the reading process with babies and young children for many reasons. When a parent holds a baby or child while reading, he or she enjoys the attention and feels loved. Books with illustrations are stimulating and activate an interest in art. Books that contain morals enhance his or her value system. Reading to a child encourages his or her imagination to rise. When children develop a love for being read to, they will desire to become readers themselves.

Fostering reading independence involves a child's cognitive, emotional, and physical development. The following list provides suggestions for parents to draw from to help children to become independent readers while fulfilling their developmental needs:

- Because your child's reading growth demands good physical condition, be sure to have his or her hearing and vision checked regularly.
- Read with your child at least once each day in some way.
- Have your child explain his or her reading program to you regularly. Play the role of the patient listener and curious questioner.
- Recognize newly acquired reading skills, and praise your child for developing them.

- Monitor your child's progress. Ask your child to read aloud. Ask him or her to read something he or she has written to you. Contact your child's teacher for an update on his or her progress.
- Be sure your child maintains a regular attendance record at school. If he or she must miss some quality school time, be sure to contact your child's teacher(s) for the work missed. Help your child to make up the assignments at home.
- Encourage your child to complete assignments, read books, think independently, be curious, and read for ideas. Help your child to study by providing space, time, and tools needed for the lessons.
- If your child is having difficulty with any part of the reading program, contact his or her teacher for suggestions, and try to help early on.
- If your child is experiencing difficulty, refrain from comparing him or her unfavorably with some other child who is quickly picking up reading skills. Remember that your child is an individual with his or her own private timeline for learning to read and to do anything else that involves a maturing process.
- To promote independent thinking, use good judgment when helping with homework. Express interest when questions are asked, and try to ask questions that will help your child find the answer. Avoid providing the answer for your child.
- Encourage your child to participate in reading events such as book fairs and completing optional projects for reading and language arts classes.
- Take your child to the library regularly. Allow your child to apply for a library card to take out books. Help your child to obtain meaning from books, properly care for books while in his or her possession, and be responsible for returning the books on time. Be aware that library cards are issued as soon as a child can sign his or her name.
- Help your child to select reading material that matches his or her interests. Respect your child's choices as long as the material is appropriate.
- Regularly read to your child, regardless of age. Set aside time every day if possible. Read a chapter or an article from a newspaper each day. Take turns reading because this encourages listening and thinking skills. Ask questions to strengthen comprehension.
- Tell your child stories, or ask him or her to tell you a story. Better yet, make up a story together. Tell stories that pass on family values or family history.
- Keep a variety of reading materials around to read, including newspapers, comic books, travel folders, recipes, various pamphlets, magazines, department store flyers, paperbacks, storybooks, and television guides.
- Encourage your child to save money and subscribe to an appropriate magazine. Examine the magazines on display in your local library for ideas.

- Regularly sit down with your child and explore the many sections of the newspaper. Discuss a different section together each night, or point out an important current event. Plan some weekend family activities using the newspaper.
- Start a family reading hour in which everyone can participate. If your family is large, choose a book or newspaper article that can be read aloud.
- Persuade your child to keep track of all the books he or she reads in one year, for example, in the form of a journal, reading log, or notebook.
- Before selecting books for birthdays or Christmas, ask your child's teacher for advice. Remember that librarians and bookstore workers can also be helpful because they will recommend books that are tailored for your child's age group and reading level.
- Ask your child to draw pictures of what he or she is reading because this will illustrate his or her perceptions of the book as well as the level of comprehension.
- Encourage your child to write his or her own short storybooks with illustrations. Try writing one together.
- When you go places and do things, take your child with you, and talk about the experiences. Be aware that such experiences will add to his or her background knowledge and vocabulary.
- Give your child opportunities for writing as well, for example, taking messages, creating shopping lists, creating cards, and writing thank you notes.
- Be a good reading role model for your child. Let your child see you reading often from books, magazines, and the newspaper.

Reading extends beyond the walls of the classroom. Parental involvement is critical for children to learn to read and sustain what they have learned. Family structures and family dynamics have changed. Parents should choose the activities and strategies that best fit in with their lifestyles and the needs of their children and attempt to try a new one on a regular basis. They will contribute toward making children more independent through reading.

Parents regularly ask for information regarding the best books for children and adolescents to read. While many school districts provide students and their families with summer reading lists, reading is a year-round necessity, and parents still desire knowledge of appropriate books throughout the school year. Here are some suggestions.

The American Library Association (ALA) provides a wealth of information on books for all ages. This organization is easily accessible through the Internet. Their website is current and updated regularly. Many libraries and bookstores can also furnish the information provided by the website to parents without Internet access.

The ALA houses the Association for Library Services to Children (ALSC) and the Young Adult Library Service Association (YALSA). The ALSC publishes Notable Children's Books, and YALSA publishes Best Books for Young Adults yearly. The titles span a variety of subjects of books written on a broad range of reading levels. The ALA also provides the Teen Guide for Parents and Caregivers.

Each year, the International Reading Association (IRA) compiles book titles for their Choices Booklists. Children, young adults, teachers, and librarians from the United States choose their favorite books. These titles become a part of the Choices Booklists and are used in classrooms, libraries, and homes to assist young readers in selecting books. Lists are published in the fall in IRA journals and may be downloaded from their website for free.

Children's Choices consists of reviews of approximately one hundred titles recommended by children. Young Adults' Choices includes descriptions of approximately 30 books selected by teen reviewers. Teachers' Choices names approximately 30 books rated by teams consisting of teachers, librarians, and reading specialists. These books are more suitable for school curriculum use.

School Library Journal is a comprehensive review source for books, multimedia, and technology for children and teens. They name and endorse a Best Books for the year list that is frequently used by elementary, junior high, and high school librarians.

The National Education Association (NEA) selects 100 books each year as great reads for children and young people. They break down the books according to age: Books for All Ages, Books for Preschoolers, Books for Children Ages 4–8, Books for Children Ages 9–12, and Books for Young Adults.

Teachers, parents, and students can utilize the lists provided by these organizations. In addition to professional organizations, parents and educators can seek out reading resources provided by colleges and universities that teach children and adolescent literature courses.

Still another source to tap into is an expert in the field of children and young adult literature. Kathleen Odean is a nationally recognized expert frequently recommended to parents and educators. Kathleen Odean travels extensively throughout the United States, conducting lectures and workshops for parents, teachers, and librarians about books for young people and how to encourage reading. She has authored *Great Books for Babies and Toddlers*, *Great Books for Boys*, and *Great Books for Girls*. These books are worthwhile resources for parents and educators.

Another area of concern expressed by parents and educators is the subject of summer reading. Parents and educators recognize its value and search for ways to motivate young people to engage in the reading process during the summer. Summer reading offers many benefits and is especially useful for maintaining skills taught during the school year.

Researchers have long studied the impact of summer reading setback on young readers. Summer reading setback takes place when students return to school after summer vacation with decreased reading skills, most likely from a lack of reading practice.

Data consistently reveal that the strongest explanation for poor reading achievement is summer reading setback. Studies further reveal that the best readers read the most and poor readers read the least. Reading builds a strong vocabulary and improves the understanding of complex written language and text grammar. As children read more, they improve fluency, increase their vocabulary, and enhance their comprehension.

The summer vacation period consists of nearly one-third of an academic year. It is imperative that children read as much as possible, even if they are not in school. Children who read during the summer are less likely to be affected by summer reading setback and more likely to experience a rate of reading achievement that remains steady or increases.

Many schools provide students and families with summer reading lists that suggest appropriate books to choose from during the summer months. Some experts report that there is a growing trend to include more modern literature along with the classics into summer reading for high school students who want to feel connected to the literature they are reading. Many districts now make summer reading a requirement that students are responsible for fulfilling and held accountable for at the start of the new school year.

What follows are some reading tips for parents to use to engage their children in reading activities during the summer that will keep them connected to reading and not suffer from a loss of reading skills when school resumes.

Read with your child. Make reading part of your daily routine. Share items like books, magazines, the newspaper, menus, TV guides, and signs found in various locations. When choosing books, look for books at an appropriate reading level and interest level. A library is a great place to find those books. If your child does not have a library card, apply for one, and use it as often as possible.

Share your reading experiences with your child. Tell about the books you enjoyed as a child. Tell about the books you enjoy reading now. Children look up to their parents. Acting as a strong reading role model sends a message that reading is enjoyable and important.

Take your child to new places, and provide new experiences. These experiences will broaden your child's knowledge when reading. Have paper, pencils, and crayons handy to give your child opportunities to write. Encourage your child to write about new experiences, make up stories and poems, or keep a journal.

Carry a book bag with you to occupy your child whenever you have to wait somewhere. This will strengthen reading ability and skills at the same time. Encourage older children to choose and read novels on an ongoing basis and to take them along whenever they leave the house.

Motivating children to read during the summer can be especially challenging. Involving youngsters in library programs is one way to meet the challenge. Libraries often provide young people with activities that accompany recommended reads during the summer months and school vacation weeks. They are also places that can provide some social interaction, and peers can gather to discuss and share what they are reading.

If attending a summer reading program is not an option, plenty of worthwhile activities can be accomplished with books at home. Here are 10 ways to get the family involved to share a book:

• Make a diorama, a three-dimensional scene set in a realistic background, to represent a favorite part of a book. Use a shoebox to create a diorama.
• Design a bookmark to capture the theme of a book.
• Create a book mobile using a hanger, string, and colorful cardboard pieces. Have the parts represent the characters, the setting, and favorite scenes from a book.
• Write a short play based on a book. Have members of the family assume the roles and act it out.
• Make a poster to advertise a book. Use a catchy slogan to get people's attention, and be sure to include the title and author of the book.
• Make a puppet to represent one of the characters of a book, or sketch a favorite character on paper. List a detailed description of the character on the back of the paper.
• Write a letter recommending a book to a friend.
• Write a different ending for a book.
• Make a timeline of major events in a book.
• Draw a favorite scene from a book.

It is the hope of educators to produce students who are independent thinkers and self-sufficient. It has been shown that reading fosters independence over time. Opportunities for strengthening reading ability must extend beyond institutions of learning. Families who attend programs that promote reading and take advantage of information provided by the school to assist their children at home not only build reading capacity, but also strengthen the family unit.

Parents need to join with educators and convey a strong message to children that reading is important and will ultimately affect how successful they will be in life. One way to accomplish this is to engage in everyday activities that require reading as a family. Educators can help parents to recognize everyday opportunities by organizing events like family literacy nights to disseminate information. When positive partnerships form, the rewards for children are endless.

Chapter 10

Celebrating Diversity

As more and more families immigrate to the United States from all parts of the world, cultural diversity becomes a natural topic to be addressed in schools, neighborhoods, and the workplace. With the influx of immigrants and a more mobile society, there is a significant shift in the makeup of the American population.

It was predicted almost 20 years ago that minorities in the United States would comprise almost one-half of the population in many metropolitan areas. Further, it was predicted that African Americans and Hispanics would constitute a majority of the school-age population and Native Americans and Asian immigrants would immigrate to some suburban and rural communities. These predictions have materialized in the twenty-first century.

Currently, Latinos represent the largest minority group in the United States as well as the fastest-growing portion of the school-age population. Yet, they are the least educated of all major ethnic groups with only approximately 12 percent earning a bachelor's degree.

According to the Census Bureau, the minority population in the United States will become the majority by the year 2100. Non-Hispanic whites will comprise 40 percent of the population in this country. The changes in the makeup of inhabitants present challenges as well as benefits for the entire population.

Diversity presents challenges that are often viewed as problematic. A common belief is that diversity causes conflict in schools and neighborhoods. Frequently, newcomers are not accepted because it is presumed they are incapable of adapting to the culture that already exists in schools and neighborhoods. In addition, the arrival of new groups, particularly minorities, leads to racial conflict and the unleashing of various forms of prejudice and intolerance. People are threatened by the newcomers and react with resentment and hostility. On the part of the immigrants, a language barrier may exist that reinforces a lack of understanding.

The benefits of a diverse population are many. The Internet, 24-hour access to news broadcasts, and increased mobility have broadened our exposure to many cultures. The more we know about different cultures, the more we can understand and value them. This understanding will lead to more harmonious relationships in schools, neighborhoods, and workplaces. The impact of positive relationships is far-reaching. They can foster economic goals, enhance the pathway to world peace, and enrich the lives of those involved.

Education is the key to understanding and appreciation of different cultures. It is also the key to lessening intolerance and prejudice. Educators and parents are the instruments that can embed cultural education in the present generation and generations to come and must be proactive in their efforts.

The intent of this chapter is to increase awareness of the diverse populations present in today's schools and the impact they are having on education. This chapter will equip educators with the information they need to understand, cope with, appreciate, and celebrate diversity.

Students of all ethnic backgrounds need to learn about tolerance and accept one another for who they are. Parents can be great teachers and role models to accomplish this. This chapter will also provide parents with helpful suggestions for providing multicultural experiences, discussions that promote tolerance, and opportunities that recognize the contributions minorities can make to society.

ESSENTIALS FOR EDUCATORS

Young people who are part of different cultural and socioeconomic groups possess their own set of beliefs, attitudes, and skills. Schools limit their ability to educate these youngsters when they ignore cultural experiences, beliefs, traditions, and skills. Students of different ethnic origins can easily be mislabeled as dysfunctional because of their lifestyles, resources, and principles. A student may be competent in the home environment yet unable to perform in school because of cultural barriers.

Mislabeling of students results from poorly designed educational programs and practices that employ a one-size-fits-all model and teachers who generalize about students based on their personal limited vision of reality. Conflicts between the home and school can result with discrepancies in how children perceive the world around them, relationship building, standards for behavior, and goals for education.

To address cultural diversity in the classroom, make cultural values and beliefs the core of all classroom organization and management decisions. For this to happen, it is imperative that teachers understand the role that culture plays in human development and the educational process. Teachers need not learn about every culture; however, they should study how culture shapes beliefs about education and learning.

Culture includes values, beliefs, and knowledge that guide communities of people in their daily lives. Educators can better address cultural diversity in the educational process when they acquire an understanding of how culture shapes educational beliefs.

Multicultural education is about social change within our society. Critical thinking, imagination, and commitment to the future are essential to its success. New questions arise, and new directions to follow uncover human potential and possibilities for the twenty-first century. Educators can utilize all students' abilities and talents to make this happen.

Presently, the mission of educators is to help all students achieve. The federal No Child Left Behind Act of 2001 maintains that all students succeed, regardless of their language or ethnic background. Schools are expected to make adequate yearly progress (AYP) and achieve goals for all student populations, including major ethnic or racial groups, economically disadvantaged students, limited English proficient (LEP) students, and students with disabilities.

The most effective means to reach a variety of populations is for educators to create an environment where all children feel valued and all children can learn. This can be accomplished if educators structure their teaching practices to acknowledge different perspectives. In addition, factors such as ensuring that students have a proper place to study, nutritious meals, and needed support may be necessary to consider.

Close attention must be given to the preschool and primary years in a child's life. These years are critical if children are to be successful in school. A high-quality preschool experience should include criteria that meet licensing standards for early childhood programs and promote collaboration between schools and social services to provide family resources, health care, and other support services to a broader range of individuals.

Numerous studies indicate that programs offering early learning experiences that provide comprehensive services to students and their families are most effective. School districts that furnish a continuing safety net of support for disadvantaged students are more likely to reduce the wide achievement gaps that currently exist and improve student learning.

Populations comprised of a variety of ethnic backgrounds have emerged throughout the world. Separate societies with many differences have developed over time and have survived those differences. Many of those differences in traditions and customs still exist today and have become interwoven in our society.

Currently, it is difficult to find a classroom in the United States that does not include students of a difference race. With these students come variations in dress, language, morals, philosophies, lifestyles, and communication skills. Students who maintain their native language at home have the opportunity to become multilingual.

The way students understand texts and language is rooted in their cultural, social, and historical backgrounds. Allowing students to use their native language in school may enhance the learning process. Inviting students to bring their home language into the classroom creates an instructional climate that welcomes all students' languages and has academic benefits. For example, students enjoy learning languages. A different student could be asked to teach a word, sentence, or song in his or her native tongue to the entire class on a regular basis. Both teacher and classmates will acquire knowledge of a new language.

Allowing students who share the same language to work together on assignments or collaborate on projects will improve their progress. Expanding school and classroom libraries to include more bilingual books and resources, providing materials in students' languages, and utilizing pictograms to communicate information are other ways to reach multicultural students and provide enriching experiences for others.

Sending information home and posting information for parents and students in a variety of languages on the school website are enormously beneficial. By doing so, educators tell families that they are respected, their input is valued, and their participation is welcomed.

Many students and their families are fearful they will lose their identities. The increasing presence of the United States in the global market increases this anxiety. Educators can create opportunities to ensure that this does not happen by making students and their families feel valued and respected for their heritage.

In order to provide the optimum educational experiences for all cultures in a given classroom, it is important for parents to become involved in the process. Every effort should be made to make parents feel welcome and to include them in their youngster's education at all levels. Educators can create hospitable situations by learning about a family's heritage, beliefs, and customs.

Many parents with different ethnic backgrounds may feel uneasy about participating in the educational process. They may not feel confident, or they may have suffered poor educational experiences as a student. Formal communication coupled with informal communication can set parents at ease and increase their willingness to become involved educationally.

Schools should be the cornerstone of cultural diversity and can initiate opportunities to celebrate it. All students will need to learn how to interact in a diverse environment. There are a variety of measures that educators and parents can engage in with young people. These strategies present a collaborative effort to encourage a sincere appreciation of cultural diversity. They will not only help all students to succeed academically, but also help them to get along with each other.

- Multicultural education must be ongoing in schools. Educators should maintain regular communication with parents. Parents are more likely to follow up on what is happening at school when they are kept informed. Telephone calls, informal meetings, e-mails, progress reports, and home visits when appropriate, will help parents to feel engaged in the educational process.
- Most parents are eager to help their children succeed in school when given the opportunity. Culturally aware teachers in no way assume that parents understand the education system in a new country. They should reach out to parents in culturally appropriate ways. Evening training sessions can be held to instruct parents on how to monitor their children's progress, advocate on their behalf, and prepare them for continuing education. If possible, translators should be present to assist with language needs.
- To determine more about what parents need, distribute surveys in parents' native languages. Make them easy to respond to. Design the surveys to collect information on ways that parents believe the school can help them become more involved in the educational process. Survey questions can also generate information about ways parents are already supporting their youngsters academically.
- Gather contact information from parents. Determine what days and times are best for the majority of parents to attend events. Consider providing multilingual newsletters to inform parents of upcoming activities and events. Assess parents' knowledge of the Internet as well as access to the World Wide Web. Consider offering training on how to use a computer and navigate through the Internet.
- Educators need professional development to properly address the many cultures existing in their schools and educate a greater range of students. Arrange workshops for faculty and staff, and make attendance mandatory. Choose a professional who is knowledgeable in the field of cultural diversity to conduct the sessions. Ask the presenter to remain available throughout the school year to faculty, staff, and parents as a resource when advice or help is needed.

- Mandate teachers incorporate the principles of cultural diversity acquired through professional development workshops into their lesson plans, and hold them accountable. Important messages are conveyed to students through what is and is not taught.
- Today's educators should attempt to shed old practices and modify traditional beliefs to truly embrace diversity and adopt new schools of thought that assert all students are valued for who they are. Although this is a challenging feat that may meet with resistance, it is worth it. Such practices encompass more students and generate a climate that breeds tolerance.
- Parents can also be included in professional development experiences. Some parents may be willing to serve as presenters who convey the various traditions and practices within their cultures. This can be accomplished informally to make parents feel more comfortable.
- Consider a formal plan for incorporating cultural diversity. Some school districts establish a policy to deal with issues of diversity and tolerance. Educators, school board members, parents, and members of the community join forces to develop, implement, and enforce compliance with the policy.
- Teachers can draw on the experiences of their students to become more informed and better appreciate different cultures. One of the most powerful ways students can share their knowledge is through stories. Provide time for students' storytelling traditions. Begin with informal oral stories and then call upon them to compose stories that sound and look more formal.
- Provide culturally different students with an environment where they know their stories will not be used in negative ways against them. Instead, create an atmosphere where they feel proud of their roots and empowered to share who they are.
- Acquire and display books about the experiences of immigrant children and their families. Such books will make immigrant children in the classroom feel more welcomed and serve as learning tools for the other members of the class.
- Assess the background knowledge of culturally diverse students, and use it to help them better understand curricular content. This background knowledge adds texture to the classroom community.
- Many multicultural students will have specific learning needs. Various learning styles should be addressed through the curriculum. Teachers can determine the learning styles of their students by considering such factors as small group instruction versus whole class instruction or visual, auditory, and kinesthetic ways of learning. Then assess how individual students will learn best and make every attempt to present academics in that way.
- Use assessments that are more authentic in nature. This will ensure that culturally diverse students are evaluated more fairly. Assessments should

focus on each student's unique responses to experiences. Multiple methods and samples should be obtained over time to achieve an accurate picture of a student's strengths and weaknesses. Minority students will feel a greater sense of responsibility for their academic performance.

- Curriculum content should acknowledge the contributions and perspectives of all groups. Guided reading about various cultures can help. The social studies curriculum often addresses different cultures. Teachers may wish to focus on the different cultures in the classroom when they materialize in the curriculum.
- The history of prejudice should be present in the curriculum at all grade levels and emphasized on meaningful occasions like Martin Luther King Day. His famous "I Have a Dream" speech could be utilized to educate students on the meaning of prejudice and its consequences.
- Students should engage in discussions that enhance the understanding of all cultures. Time could be allotted for students to complete and present projects that address their own ethnic backgrounds. Students should be given the opportunity to ask questions of each other and compare the cultures presented.
- Speakers from different cultures within the community could be invited to speak to the student population. Communities have rich resources that can enhance cultural diversity. Consider monthly meetings where representatives from different cultures could address both parents and students.
- Differences in ethnicity can be celebrated through venues like international nights, literacy nights, family nights, and dramatic presentations honoring various cultures.
- Cultural awareness nights are instrumental in bringing families of all ethnicities together. Families are asked to set up booths displaying posters and maps that depict their culture. Dressing in traditional clothing and sharing traditional foods are encouraged. Music, dancing, artwork, and crafts representing their native lands may be displayed.
- Workshops could be conducted at schools to address the needs of newcomers to the community. Topics for the workshops could include finance, community resources, ESL resources, literacy, understanding the school structure and community, and technology.
- Encourage students to research different ethnic groups using technology and share their findings with the class.
- When students work cooperatively in the classroom, create groups that reflect diversity.

Today's educators must make a commitment to recognize and learn about cultural diversity in order to reach all students academically and support them emotionally and socially. Engaging in practices that transform educators into leaders of multicultural education benefit all students. Students of various ethnic origins attain a sense of belonging. Other members of the student body enhance their knowledge of different cultures and learn to accept differences. Students improve socially and interact with each other more positively.

As a starting point, learn to pronounce each student's name correctly. Meet with students individually. Allow them to share both good and bad experiences they encountered because of their ethnic background. Coordinate round table discussions with students to share their backgrounds, traditions, and family values with each other. Teachers are encouraged to contribute to the discussion by telling about their own heritage.

Some educators assume all immigrant families have the same backgrounds and deal with the same issues. Educators should be conscious of their own biases and be careful not to relay them through actions and when speaking with students. Biases emerge from an individual's own culture, background, and life experiences. Invite constructive criticism when sharing perceptions of different cultures. Teach students to do this in a respectful way. Point out how stereotypes that target individual ethnic groups can be insulting and hurtful.

Build a community of educators who are from different cultures. These communities can provide enriching life experiences where members can learn from one another. Socialize with each other. Share traditions and family stories from long ago. These experiences will be helpful when educators attempt to apply them to the classroom.

As educators, never stop being students of cultural diversity. Be conscious of the cultures present in classrooms. Invite discussion from students. Learn from culturally diverse students. Encourage them to be who they are through projects and assignments. Serve as a role model for students. Respect and celebrate differences.

Classrooms are places where students from a variety of backgrounds coexist. Providing experiences for all students to share the components of their heritage will enhance the learning of all. It will give culturally diverse students a sense of belonging and create a classroom environment that includes tolerance and acceptance. Learning about students' lives outside of the classroom will enable teachers to tailor instruction to meet their needs.

Today's educators cannot view multicultural students as a problem. The one-size-fits-all model of instruction is no longer effective. When culturally and linguistically diverse students are educated using a multifaceted approach to meet their needs, parents are more likely to join with the school as a partner in their children's education. Adapting instruction and assessment to accommodate new populations of students is cumbersome but worth it when the benefits materialize in the students.

PRACTICES FOR PARENTS

Parents are a key element when teaching children about cultural diversity. Parents have a strong influence on how their children will perceive and treat individuals of different ethnic origins. They can make their children aware of the beauty in the differences of others, or they can promote prejudice forms of thinking and behavior.

As parents, determine your beliefs about cultural diversity and tolerance and why you have adopted them. Your goal should be to teach your children about different cultures, especially the different ways people live and why. Be careful not to project your biases on them. Encourage them to be open to new experiences. Children emulate their parents. If your actions reflect tolerance and acceptance, theirs will, too. Steer their development in a direction that is healthy, open to new situations, and nonjudgmental of others.

Realizing similarities and differences among people typically begins at home by noticing members of the family. Awareness of differences helps children gain a sense of their own identity. As soon as children are aware of their environment, they can be introduced to diversity and its benefits.

Toddlers become conscious of race and skin color and are able to learn the names for specific ethnic groups. They do not, however, fully understand the meaning of labels. Preschoolers can identify their own racial or ethnic group. They may even begin to view their own group or other groups positively or negatively. Feelings about groups are usually formed by absorbing messages emitted by parents, society, the media, literature, and even toys. Seven- through eleven-year-olds have a stronger understanding of their own racial and ethnic identity and will seek to determine what it means to be a member of a group.

Parents can do a number of things with their children to enhance their understanding of diversity and learn to appreciate differences in the world.

Begin by providing a safe environment where differences can be discussed and information can be provided to explain the nature of stereotypes and address problems that arise when individuals of different origins are labeled. Providing opportunities for children to play with other youngsters from different cultures and backgrounds allows them to become used to differences and discover that these cultural differences do not impact relationships negatively. Choose places like schools, camps, childcare facilities, and sports' teams with diverse populations.

Another way to increase exposure to various ethnicities is to attend cultural festivals and celebrations. They are often fun. New foods, forms of dress, dancing, customs, and languages can be experienced. The local newspaper will advertise events taking place in nearby communities. The Internet is another good source to use to locate the times and places of such events. The Internet can help families pinpoint particular ethnic festivals and celebrations that they may want to attend.

Openly discuss comments that your children and teens make that reflect prejudice. Answer questions they have about prejudice. Emphasize that prejudice is the opposite of tolerance. Prejudice individuals are not accepting of others. Individuals who practice tolerance are. Make it known, as a parent, that you welcome questions about different cultures. Be willing to study cultures your family is interested in. The differences that come from people all over the world contribute new ideas and enrich the culture of the United States.

Part of today's child rearing practices involves preparing young people to live, learn, and work in communities that will become even more diverse with time. Young people who learn to be tolerant and accepting of differences in others will be awarded more opportunities in education, business, and life.

Parents who adopt children of another race need to discuss the differences that exist within the family unit they are now a part of and show acceptance for the differences. Adopted children must also be taught how to deal with racially derogatory comments that may be spoken outside of the home. These children should be allowed to practice customs and traditions that make them who they are. They should also be allowed to celebrate holidays that are pertinent to their culture, along with the holidays celebrated in their new home.

Be mindful that children learn from their parents. The opinions that are expressed and demonstrated at home are handed down to the children who very often express them in outside situations. Young children who use racial slurs are usually repeating what they observed others say in anger or fear during times of conflict. When this occurs, identify the main problem and help children understand that it does not involve another person's heritage or skin color. As children become older, make it clear that racial attacks, verbal or physical, will not be allowed. It is critical to convey that no one is superior over another because of race.

Tolerance involves an open attitude toward others and respect for the differences that exist among others. These differences can extend to gender, race, mental and physical disabilities, and other differences that set individuals apart from others. Tolerating others, however, does not include hurtful behaviors. Actions involving insulting remarks, lying, cheating, stealing, and bullying should never be tolerated.

Parents can teach tolerance in a variety of ways. Begin by correcting your own stereotypic beliefs and model respect toward others. Be aware of what you say in front of youngsters.

Select reading material, music, movies, art, and toys that are free of discrimination and prejudice. Acknowledge and discuss differences in others with respect, starting with members of the family. Such differences can extend to abilities, talents, interests, and styles. The results will enable children to feel accepted, respected, and valued. These feelings will transfer to the way children treat others.

Be a strong role model. Interact socially with people of different cultures. Join international groups in your area. Explain your choices, and attend appropriate gatherings as a family.

Invite a family with a different ethnic background to dinner. This demonstrates a commitment to accept others for who they are and a willingness to associate with them freely. Encourage your guests to bring a dish that reflects their heritage.

As a family, visit restaurants that serve ethnic food. Encourage all family members to be adventurous when selecting food choices from the menu.

Visit the local library and bookstores. Select books about various cultures, and read them together. Try to find a new fact about a different country or culture each week. Use a journal to collect the facts. As a family, create a collage to represent the different ethnic groups or countries that you studied together. Compare and contrast the findings.

Watch documentaries and informational programs about different countries or heritages together on television and discuss them.

Celebrating the differences of others does not mean abandoning your own family's heritage. As a family, study your own cultural traditions. Trace your heritage back to your ancestors. Create a family tree. Many families can trace their histories back to immigrant ancestors who traveled great distances from their native lands. Discuss risks and hardships they faced as well as the new freedoms they acquired in their new country. Children are fascinated by their ancestry and enjoy researching their roots.

It is important for parents to be aware of the impact they have on their children and adolescents regarding cultural diversity. Modeling respectful behavior toward multicultural groups and providing enriching experiences that expose young people to the differences in the makeup of society will provide the skills needed to value the unique contributions that culturally diverse groups make.

The population of children and adolescents from immigrant families is growing faster than any other group of youngsters in the nation. It is important for both educators and parents to react responsibly toward the issues brought about by new populations who are culturally diverse. Because schools are the likely place where various cultures will first meet, it is imperative that educators take the lead in discovering ways to make the interactions among children, parents, and teachers into positive experiences.

America continues to be the melting pot of the world. All young people should feel good about where they came from and who they are. Parents can work with other parents and educators to generate a positive perspective of the differences present in various cultures. Such partnerships can provide learning experiences that move young people from tolerance to acceptance. Such partnerships bring about a more harmonious society.

Afterword

It has been my intent to unite educators and parents in the education process with the publication of this book. In order for children to achieve academic success and grow into adults who are prepared to function in and contribute to society, educators and parents must work together. Both educators and parents have the best interest of children at hand. Both educators and parents want children to complete their education equipped with the knowledge and skills to be productive as adults. This can be achieved with the formation of a partnership.

Educators and parents have certain roles to fulfill. When both partners fulfill their obligations, the results are positive. If either partner fails in his duties, the results are negative.

I would like to conclude the text with a poem I feel best sums up my purpose. It illustrates how a meaningful partnership between a teacher and parent can shape a child and how proud each partner is of his contribution. I believe partnerships offer promising results.

Unity

I dreamed I stood in a studio
And watched two sculptors there.
The clay they used was a young child's mind
And they fashioned it with care.

One was a teacher; the tools she used were
Books and music and art;
One, a parent with a guiding hand
And a gentle loving heart.

125

Day after day the teacher toiled,
With a touch that was deft and sure,
While the parent labored by his side
And polished and smoothed it o'er.

And when at last their task was done
They were proud of what they had wrought,
For the things they had molded into the child
Could neither be sold or bought.

And each agreed he would have failed
If he had worked alone.
For behind the parent stood the school,
And behind the teacher the home.

—Anonymous

References

Aftab, P. *Stop cyberbullying*. WiredKids, Inc. www.stopcyberbullying.org/educators/ guide_for_schools.html (accessed April 16, 2010).

Agirdag, O. 2009. All languages welcomed here. *Educational Leadership* 66(7): 20–25.

Alverman, D. 2002. Effective literacy instruction for adolescents. *Journal of Literacy Research* 34: 189–208.

Armstrong, T. 1995. *The myth of the ADD child*. New York: A Dutton Book, Penguin Group.

Azzam, A. 2005. Reading at risk. *Educational Leadership* 63(2): 88.

Baker, M. 2002. Reading resistance in middle school: What can be done? *Journal of Adolescent and Adult Literacy* 45: 364–366.

Barth, R. 1980. *Run school run*. Cambridge: Harvard University Press.

Barton, P. 2006. The dropout problem: Losing ground. *Educational Leadership* 63(5): 14–18.

Beane, A. 1999. *The bully-free classroom*. Minneapolis: Free Spirit Publishing.

Beane, A. 2009. *Bullying prevention for schools: A step-by-step guide to implementing a successful anti-bullying program*. San Francisco: Josey-Bass.

Bennett, C. 1986. *Comprehensive multicultural education, theory, and practice*. Boston: Allyn & Bacon.

Ben-Yosef, E. 2003. Respecting student cultural literacies. *Educational Leadership* 61(2): 80–82.

Biancarosa, G. 2005. After third grade. *Educational Leadership* 63(2): 16–22.

Blachowicz, C., and P. Fisher. 2004. Vocabulary lessons. *Educational Leadership*, 66(6): 66–69.

Bowman, B. *Cultural diversity and academic achievement*. North Central Regional Educational Laboratory. www.ncrel.org/sdrs/areas/issues/educatrs/leadrshp/le0bow.htm (accessed April 28, 2010).

Blum, R. 2005. A case for school connectedness. *Educational Leadership* 62(7): 16–20.

Bresman, D., A. Erdmann, and K. Olson. 2009. A learning community blossoms. *Educational Leadership* 66(8): 68–71.

Butler, K. 1984. *Learning and teaching style in theory and practice.* Maynard, Mass.: Gabriel Systems, Inc.

Butler, K. 1995. *Learning styles, personal exploration, and practical applications: An introduction to style for secondary students.* Columbia, Conn.: The Learners Dimension.

Camilli, G., and P. Wolfe. 2004. Research on reading: A cautionary tale. *Educational Leadership* 61(6): 26–29.

Clark, B. 2006. Breaking through to reluctant readers. *Educational Leadership* 63(5): 66–69.

Claxton, C. 1990. Learning styles, minority students, and effective education. *Journal of Developmental Education* 14: 6–8, 35.

Coiro, J. 2005. Making sense of online text. *Educational Leadership* 63(2): 30–35.

Campano, G. 2007. Honoring student stories. *Educational Leadership* 65(2): 48–54.

Constantino, S. 2003. *Engaging all families.* Lanham, Md.: Rowman & Littlefield Publications.

Cooper, H. 2001. Homework for all in moderation. *Educational Leadership* 68(7): 34–38.

Coutant, C., and N. Perchemlides. 2005. Strategies for teen readers. *Educational Leadership* 63(2): 42–47.

Cox, B., and M. Ramirez. 1981. Cognitive styles: Implications for multicultural education. In *Education in the 80s*, ed. J. Banks. Washington, DC: National Education Association.

Crary, E. 2004. *Children and the Internet.* Seattle: Parenting Press.

Crosnoe, R., and B. Needham. 2004. Holism, contextual variability, and the study of friendships in adolescent development. *Journal-Child Development* 75(1). The Society for Research in Child Development, Inc. www.keepkidshealthy.com/adolescent/adolescetnquicktips/peerpressure.html (accessed August 10, 2007).

Cushman, K. 2006. Help us care enough to learn. *Educational Leadership* 63(5): 34–37.

Darling-Hammond, L., and O. Ifill-Lynch. 2006. If they'd only do their work! *Educational Leadership* 63(5): 8–13.

Decker, L., and V. Decker. 2001. *Engaging families & communities: Pathways to educational success.* Fairfax, Va.: Decker & Associates.

Decker, L., and V. Decker. 2002. *Home, school, and community partnerships.* Lanham, Md.: Rowman & Littlefield Publications.

Decker, L., G. Gregg, and V. Decker. 1994. *Getting parents involved in their children's education.* Lanham, Md.: Rowman & Littlefield Publications.

Dunn, R. 1997. The goals and track record of multicultural education. *Educational Leadership* 14(7): 74–77.

Duke, N. 2004. The case for informational text. *Educational Leadership* 61(6): 40–44.

Elkind, D. 1981. *The hurried child: Growing up too fast too soon.* Reading, Mass.: Addison Wesley Publishing Co.

Epstein, J.L., and F. VanVoorhis. 2000. *Teachers involve parents in schoolwork: Interactive homework.* Johns Hopkins University: National Network of Partnership Schools.

Epstein, J.L. et al. 2009. *School, family, and community partnerships: Your handbook for Action*, 3rd ed. Thousand Oaks, Calif.: Corwin Press.

ERIC Clearinghouse on Urban Education. *A guide to choosing an afterschool program.* New York: Teachers College, Columbia University.

ERIC Clearinghouse on Urban Education. *Helping parents help their children learn.* New York: Teachers College, Columbia University.

Frankfurter, F. 1949. Dennis v. US. *US Report* 339: 184.

2002. From sanctions to solutions: Meeting the needs of low-performing schools. Alexandria, Va.: National Association of State Boards of Education.

Gagnon, P. 1995. What should children learn? *The Atlantic Monthly* 276(6): 65–78.

Gandara, P. 2010. The Latino education crisis. *Educational Leadership* 67(5): 24–30.

Garcia, E., B. Jensen, and K. Scribner. 2009. The demographic imperative. *Educational Leadership* 66(7): 8–13.

Gardner, H. 1991. *The unschooled mind: How children think and how schools should teach.* New York: Basic Books.

Gaskins, I. 2004. Word detectives. *Educational Leadership* 61(6): 70–73.

Get involved: How parents can help their children do better in school. www.edgov/pubs (accessed on October 27, 2007).

Glatthorn, A. 1984. *Differentiated supervision.* Alexandria, Va.: Association for Supervision and Curriculum Development.

Glazer, N., and S. Williams. 2001. Averting the homework crisis. *Educational Leadership* 58(7): 43–45.

Goldbloom, R. 2001. *Parents' primer on school bullying.* www.readersdigest.ca/mag/2001/10/bullying.html (accessed on August 29, 2007).

Goodlad, J. 1984. *A place called school: Prospects for the future.* New York: McGraw Hill Book Company.

Great Schools Staff. *How important is cultural diversity at your school?* www.greatschools.org (Accessed on April 28, 2010).

Gregorc, A. 1982a. *An adult's guide to style.* Maynard, Mass.: Gabriel Systems, Inc.

Gregorc, A. 1982b. *Gregorc style delineator: Developmental, technical, and administrative manual*, revised edition. Maynard, Mass.: Gabriel Systems, Inc.

Guild, P., and S. Garger. 1998. *Marching to a different drummer*, 2nd ed. Alexandria, Va.: Association for Supervision and Curriculum Development.

Guild, P., L. McKinney, and J. Fouts. 1990. *A study of the learning styles of elementary students: Low achievers, average achievers, high achievers.* Seattle: The Teaching Advisory.

Hale-Benson, J. 1986. *Black children: Their roots, culture, and learning styles*, revised ed. Baltimore: Johns Hopkins University Press.

Herrera, C., Z. Vang, and L. Gale. *Group mentoring: A study on mentoring groups in three programs*. Prepared for the National Mentoring Partnership's Public Policy Council. United States Department of Education Office of Educational Research and Improvement.

Hill, J., and K. Flynn. 2006. *Classroom instruction that works with English language learners*. Alexandria, Va.: Association for Supervision and Curriculum Development.

Hilliard, A. 1989. Teachers and culture styles in a pluralistic society. *NEA Today*: 65–69.

Hobbs, R. 2005. What's news? *Educational Leadership* 63(2): 58–61.

Holloway, J. 2004. Family literacy. *Educational Leadership* 66(6): 88–89.

Hoover, J.H., and R. Olicer. 1996. *The bully prevention handbook*. Bloomington, Ind.: National Education Service.

Hope School Improvement Team. 2010. *Hope elementary school Title I parental involvement policy*. Scituate, R.I.: Author.

Hutchins, D.J., M.D. Greenfeld, and J.L. Epstein. 2008. *Family reading night*. New York: Eye on Education.

Inlay, L. 2005. Safe schools for the roller coaster years. *Educational Leadership* 62(7): 41–43.

Irvine, J., and D. York. 1995. Learning styles and culturally diverse students: A literature review. In *Handbook of research on multicultural education*, eds. J. Banks and C. Banks. New York: Macmillan.

Ivey, G., and M. Baker. 2004. Phonics instruction for older students? Just say no. *Educational Leadership* 61(6): 35–39.

Ivey, G., and D. Fisher. 2005. Learning from what doesn't work. *Educational Leadership* 63(2): 8–14.

Juel, C., and R. Deffes. 2004. Making words stick. *Educational Leadership* 61(6): 30–34.

Katz, L. 1995. *How can we strengthen children's self-esteem?* ACCESS ERIC. www.kidsource.com/kidsource/content2/strengthen_children_self.html (Accessed August 22, 2009).

Kennedy, R. *Fostering cultural diversity in your school*. http://privateschool.about.com/cs/administrators/a/diversity.html (Accessed on April 28, 2010).

Kowalski, R., S. Limber, and P. Agatston. 2007. *Cyber bullying: Bullying in the digital age*. Malden, Mass.: Blackwell Publishers.

Landsman, J. 2006. *White teachers/Diverse classrooms*. Washington, DC: Stylus Press.

Leong, P. 2002. Children's literature offers lessons in decision-making. Ohio University Extension Fact Sheet HYG-5290–95. www.ohioline.osu.edu/hyg-fact/5000/5290.html (Accessed on July 26, 2007).

Louv, R. 2005. *Lost child in the woods: Saving our children from nature-deficit disorder*. Chapel Hill: Algonquin Books of Chapel Hill.

Love Our Children USA. *Bullying and guns at school.* http://loveourchildrenusa.org/bullying.php (Accessed on August 29, 2007).

Lyon, G.R., and V. Chhabra. 2004. The science of reading research. *Educational Leadership* 61(6): 12–17.

Mann, W., and J. Lash. 2004. *Test and performance anxiety.* Psychological Services Center. www.psc.uc.edu (Accessed on March 1, 2010).

Marzano, R. 2007. *The art and science of teaching: A comprehensive framework for effective instruction.* Alexandria, Va.: Association for Supervision and Curriculum Development.

Marzano, R., T. Waters, and B. McNulty. 2005. *School leadership that works.* Alexandria, Va.: Mid-continent Research for Education and Learning.

Miller, M. 2006. Where they are: Working with marginalized students. *Educational Leadership* 63(5): 50–54.

Mizelle, N. 2005. Moving out of middle school. *Educational Leadership* 62(7): 56–59.

Myers, I. 1980. Taking type into account in education. In *Psychological (Myers-Briggs) type differences in education,* 2nd ed., eds. M. McCauley and F. Natter. Gainsville, Fla.: Center for Applications of Psychological Type, Inc.

Myers, I. 1990. *Gifts differing,* 2nd ed. Palo Alto, Calif.: Consulting Psychologists Press, Inc.

Nansel, T.R., M. Overpeck, R.S. Pilla, W.J. Ruan, B. Simons-Morton, and P. Scheidt. 2001. Bullying behaviors among US youth: Prevalence and association with psychological adjustment. *Journal of the American Medical Association* 285 (16): 2094–2100.

Nemours Foundation. 2004. *A parent's guide to surviving the teen years.* www.kidshealth.org/parent/growth/growing/adolescent.html (Accessed on August 10, 2007).

Nemours Foundation. *Developing your child's self-esteem.* www.kidshealth.org/parent/emotions/feelings/selfesteem.html (Accessed on July 26, 2007).

Nemours Foundation. *Teaching your child tolerance.* http://kidshealth.org/parent/positive/talk/tolerance.html (Accessed on April 28, 2010).

O'Brien, L. 2001. *How to get good grades.* Dayton, Ohio: Woodburn Press.

Odean, K. 1998. *Great books for boys.* New York: Ballantine Books.

Odean, K. 2002. *Great books for girls,* revised ed. New York: Ballantine Books.

Odean, K. 2003. *Great books for babies and toddlers.* New York: Ballantine Books.

Ohler, J. 2007. *Digital storytelling in the classroom: New pathways to literacy, learning, and creativity.* Newbury Park, Calif.: Corwin Press.

Ohler, J. 2009. Orchestrating the media collage. *Educational Leadership* 66(6): 9–13.

Oltman, P., E. Raskin, and H. Witkin. 1971. *Group embedded figures test.* Palo Alto, Calif.: Consulting Psychologists Press, Inc.

Olweus, D. 1993. *Bullying at school: What we know and what we can do.* Cambridge: Blackwell Publishers, Inc.

Parks, A., and S. Anderson. 2002. *Ten golden rules that guide loving families.* www.teenliberty.org/parents_as_mentors.htm (Accessed on March 2, 2008).

Parks, A., and S. Anderson. 2010. *Ten golden rules that guide loving families: A parent-mentor training program.* http://teenliberty.org/TrainTrainers.htm (Accessed on April 21, 2010).

Plevyak, L. 2003. Parent involvement in education: Who decides? *The Education Digest* 69(2): 32–38.

Price, H. 2008. *Mobilizing the community to help students succeed.* Alexandria, Va.: Association for Supervision and Curriculum Development.

Price, L. 2005. The biology of risk-taking. *Educational Leadership* 62(7), 22–26.

Rabkin, N., and R. Redmond. 2004. Putting the arts in the picture. In *Putting the arts in the picture: Education in the twenty-first century,* eds. N. Rabkin and R. Redmond. Chicago: Columbia College Chicago.

Ramirez, A.Y., and I. Soto-Hinman. 2009. A place for all families. *Educational Leadership* 66(7): 79–82.

Ramirez, M. 1989. Pluralistic education: A bicognitive-multicultural model. *The Clearinghouse Bulletin* 3: 4–5.

Rasinski, T. 2004. Creating fluent readers. *Educational Leadership* 66(6): 46–51.

Reid Lyon, G., and C. Chhabra. 2004. The science of reading research. *Educational Leadership* 61(6): 13–17.

Renard, L. 2005. Teaching the DIG generation. *Educational Leadership* 62(7): 44–47.

Rhode Island Career Resource Network. *Discover your child's preferred learning style.* Cranston, R.I.: Rhode Island Department of Labor & Training.

Rhode Island Career Resource Network. *Parent involvement = student success.* Cranston, R.I.: Rhode Island Department of Labor & Training.

Rolfe, A. *Mentoring works.* http://mentoring-works.com (Accessed on April 12, 2010).

Rubinstein-Avila, E. 2006. Connecting with Latino learners. *Educational Leadership* 63(5): 38–43.

Scherer, M. 2005. Keeping adolescents in mind. *Educational Leadership* 62(7): 7.

Scituate School Department. 2010. *Strategic plan.* Scituate, R.I.: Author.

Shade, B. 1989. The influence of perpetual development on cognitive style: Cross ethnic comparisons. *Early Child Development and Care* 51: 137–155.

Shakeel, J. *Teaching our kids about cultural diversity.* More4kids. www.more4kids,info/589/teaching-kids-cuktural-diversity (Accessed on April 28, 2010).

Shute, N. 2009. The amazing teen brain. *U.S. News and World Report.*

Sizer, T. 1984. *Horace's compromise: The dilemma of the American high school.* Boston: Houghton Mifflin Company.

Sprenger, M. 2005. Inside Amy's brain. *Educational Leadership* 62(7): 28–32.

Strickland, D., and T. Shanahan. 2004. Laying the groundwork for literacy. *Educational Leadership,* 66(6): 74–77.

Strout, M. 2005. Positive behavioral support at the classroom level: Considerations and strategies. *Beyond Behavior.*

Substance Abuse and Mental Health Services Administration Center for Substance Abuse Treatment. 2007. *Getting the facts about adolescent substance abuse and treatment.* www.athealth.com/Consumer/adolescentsufacts.html (Accessed on August 10, 2007).

Tatum, A. 2005. *Teaching reading in black adolescent males: Closing the achievement gap.* Portland, ME: Stenhouse Publishers.

Taylor, J. 2006. *Raising good decision makers.* www.drjimtaylor.com/homtemplate/k-and-c-alert-06-decision-making.html (Accessed on July 26, 2007).

Test Taking Tips. www.testtakingtips.com (Accessed on March 1, 2010).

The Parent Institute. 1996. *Quick tips video: What to do if your child is having a problem in school.* Fairfax Station, Va.: The Parent Institute.

Tobias, C., and P. Guild. 1986. *No sweat! How to use your learning style to be a better student.* Seattle, Wash.: The Teaching Advisory.

Tovani, C. 2005. The power of purposeful reading. *Educational Leadership* 63(2): 48–51.

United States Department of Education. 2007. *Engaging parents in education: Lessons from five parental information and resource centers.* Jessup, Md.: WestEd.

United States Department of Education Office of Educational Research and Improvement. 1993. *Help your child improve in test taking.* www2.ed.gov/pubs/parents/TestTaking/index.html (Accessed on February 24, 2010).

Ways You Can Help Your Kids Test Better. http://shine.yahoo.com (Accessed on February 24, 2010).

Weilbacher, M. 2009. The window into green. *Educational Leadership* 66(8): 38–44.

Weinberger, S. 1992. *The mentor handbook.* Educational Resources Network, Inc. www.mentorconsultinggroup.com/pub/native_mentoring.pdf (Accessed on April 12, 2010).

Weissbourd, R. 2009. *The parents we mean to be: How well-intentioned adults undermine children's moral and emotional development.* Orlando: Houghton Mifflin Harcourt.

Weissbourd, R. 2009. The schools we mean to be. *Educational Leadership* 66(8): 26–31.

Witkin, H., C. Moore, D. Goodenough, and P. Cox. 1977. Field-dependent and field-independent cognitive styles and their educational implications. *Review of Educational Research* 47: 1–64.

Wolf, M., and M. Barzillai. 2009. The importance of deep reading. *Educational Leadership* 66(6): 33–37.

About the Author

Lisa J. Harpin has taught in a variety of capacities for 28 years. She currently teaches English and literacy at Burrillville Middle School in Harrisville, Rhode Island. She holds a bachelor of arts degree in elementary education and a master of arts degree in agency counseling from Rhode Island College. She has worked as a family counselor with families in crisis. She received a doctorate in educational leadership from Johnson & Wales University. Dr. Harpin serves as an associate student advisor and dissertation editor, and conducts writing seminars for doctoral students at Johnson & Wales University.

Breinigsville, PA USA
04 November 2010
248625BV00002B/3/P